EJ & D

DEEPERWELLS

A 5-WEEK CHALLENGE TO LIVE DEEPER IN A SHALLOW WORLD

DEDICATION

To all of our pastors, mentors, parents, and spiritual fathers and mothers who taught us how to follow Jesus with wild abandon: your example has encouraged us to put everything aside in order to live a lifestyle of depth and intimacy with God, to increase our awareness of the presence of the Holy Spirit, and to live an abundant life, full of the fruit of spiritual discipline.

Your impact is exponential.

CONTENTS

INTRODUCTION
The Problem with Shallow

*I*t doesn't have to be this way. There's so much more to this life! There's an epidemic in our communities. No, it is not a disease, or a condition, or even a political agenda. This epidemic has quietly ravaged a single people group, with many of them completely unaware of the damage done to them!

This epidemic is not widespread in the world. It is centralized and confined to Christianity, and in my experience, Western Christianity. This epidemic is *shallow Christianity*.

For some reason, many Christians in the West seem to believe that church attendance is the same as salvation; that giving in an offering is the same as personal evangelism; that singing songs on a Sunday morning is the same as having a prayer life.

There are many reasons why this shallow way of living in relationship with God has surfaced in the Church. This book is not to figure out all the reasons why we ended up here, but how do we go deeper? How do we dive past the shallow waters of apathy and immaturity and into the deep waters of spiritual intimacy and maturity?

Through our experience in ministry, we have learned that we can debate all day with people, try to persuade them and convince them intellectually that they should go deeper in their relationship with

God. Yet the moment we challenge them, some other voice speaks into their lives and convinces them—in the same, persuasive way—that they are doing great and they can be content to stay where they are.

Convincing someone to pursue God may work for a little while, but only until a better argument or justification against going deeper in their walk with God comes their way. Convincing a person to seek God is not the answer.

Leading them into an encounter with God is the solution.

The psalmist put it this way:

"Taste and see that the LORD is good..."[1]

Once you experience and partake of the presence of God, it instills a deep thirst that you were unaware of previously. That thirst drives you to have more. And the more you have of God, the more you want of Him!

DIGGING WELLS

In many countries today, we have the gift of instant access to water. We go to the faucet in our home, turn it on, and immediately have a stream of water flowing to quench our thirst. When we are not at home, all you have to do is stop at the closest gas station, fast food restaurant, or grocery store, and you can easily purchase a bottle of water.

However, this is not the case in many other countries. Water is a vital source of life that takes work to provide. In some regions of our

---

1 Psalm 34:8

world, water is so scarce that it is as valuable as gold! For thousands of years, one of the ways we have provided sources of water for ourselves and our communities has been by digging wells—holes in the ground that are constructed and sealed to contain water that is flowing deep underground, hidden from the ground's surface. It took work and great effort to utilize these wells. It was labor-intensive to dig a well. It requires an incredible effort to draw water from the well. And the location of the well was not convenient, like a house's faucet is. The well does not come to you; you go to the well!

The Bible is full of references to wells (fountains, cisterns, etc.). While many of these references deal with a real well to draw water from, the idea of a well was often used symbolically to speak about our spiritual condition—our source of life, the things we choose to satisfy our needs, etc.

In John 4, Jesus sat with a Samaritan woman who was completely broken on the inside. She came to the well Jesus was resting in the middle of the day—the worst time to draw from a well. As Jesus speaks with her, we see the depth of brokenness in this woman. She is an adulteress. She has had five husbands, and the man she was currently with was not her husband. No wonder why this woman came to the well at the worst time of day! She would have been the talk of the village. She would have developed a reputation in the community. She was the woman from whom other women would hide their husbands. She comes to the town well because she is thirsty, but comes at the worst time of day so she can avoid all the people who would judge her and condemn her. She came to a shallow well looking to satisfy a deeper thirst but would leave dissatisfied with her lukewarm water.

Little did she know that Jesus would offer her water that would forever quench her thirst—*living* water. This water is not a physical liquid, but a spiritual source of life that sustains our very being. Even though this living water is free and accessible, it also takes effort to draw. Listen to the woman's words:

> *"Sir, you have nothing to draw water with, and the well is deep…"*[2]

If she only knew that although she was talking to Jesus, she was speaking to herself as well! The well of living water is deep—it is far deeper than anything we could ever imagine. This living water is God. There is no end to the size, breadth, and depth of who He is. That means that this well has limitless depth and never runs out of its life-giving sustenance. But to access that water, you must have tools to reach deep, because this water resides far below the surface of our lives. This water is found in the depths of who God is and meant to quench the deep thirst of our souls.

Only when we drink from these deep waters of who God is will we find a life worth living, a life of strength and peace, and a life of enduring joy no matter what situations we face in this life.

The Bible speaks of the importance of drawing from this well. The prophet Isaiah wrote,

> *"'Behold, God is my salvation; I will trust, and will not be afraid; for the Lord God is my strength and my song, and he has become my salvation.' With joy you will draw water from the wells of salvation.!"*[3]

---

2 John 4:11 (ESV)
3 Isaiah 12:3 (ESV)

What was Isaiah talking about here? He was speaking about the coming of the Messiah—Jesus—and the life of salvation that He would bring to His people. God, Himself, is our salvation. And He has become the source of living water that we drink from for both life and salvation.

However, this is easier said than done. Many of our issues in the Church today are present because there are so many people who are like the Samaritan woman: they are sitting with Jesus, speaking with Jesus, yet blind to their spiritual condition. They believe they are drinking from the deep waters of who God is, but in reality, they are only drinking from the shallow waters of human effort and strength. God spoke against this through the prophet Jeremiah:

> *"My people have done two evil things: They have abandoned me—the fountain of living water. And they have dug for themselves cracked cisterns (wells) that can hold no water at all!"*[4]

Whenever we try to live as followers of Jesus in our strength, we find ourselves drawing water from broken and insufficient wells. No matter how much water you put into it, it will always be empty. It will always leave you feeling ultimately "dry." But the problem gets worse. The more you try to draw from spiritual wells dug in your own effort, the more you take on the characteristics of your well. This happens because you become like the source from which you draw. If your well is dry, you become dry. If your well is broken, you become broken. If your well is dug out of "flesh"—human effort—then you will only ever live on and produce the "flesh" in your life. The

---

4 Jeremiah 2:13 (NLT)

5

Apostle Peter described people who are like this. He called them false teachers. They were full of pride and arrogance. They call their sin and immorality "godly" and bring division and pain to churches. They are greedy, and they lie—all so they can gain your love, respect, and support. Fed up with these kinds of shallow people in the Church, Peter says:

"These people are springs without water..."[5]

The warning is clear: shallow spirituality is dangerous. It deceives you into thinking that you are mature, impressive, and worthy of respect. It fools you into thinking that you have "arrived." This deception is infused in the bitter waters of shallow spirituality. Peter later states that these people,

"...promise freedom, but they themselves are slaves of sin and corruption."[6]

So how do we guard ourselves against this kind of self-deception and self-bondage? That's a great question!

Dig deeper.

Dig deep wells that tap into the true living water. Do the hard work of disciplining yourself to dig daily and to draw from those wells daily.

In this book, you will learn the multiple wells you can dig, the

5 2 Peter 2:17
6 2 Peter 2:19 (NLT)

tools you will need to learn, and be challenged to live a deeper life with God than you have ever experienced before.

The goal is not to give you a moment or fleeting season of passion for God. Instead, the goal is to help you construct solid wells that will be reliable for you; wells that you can draw from daily for the rest of your life; wells that will let you drink deeply from the true source of life: Jesus Christ.

So as you take up this challenge, commit yourself to set aside time daily to walk through these daily devotional pages. Resolve in your heart and mind right now that you are going to see this through to the end. There will be times where it may get tough and challenging, but make this a priority.

In the back of this book is a section that provides practical tools to develop a daily routine and rhythm to help you drink deeply from the presence of God.

Lastly, understand that you're not reading a book. You're using a tool that will help create an atmosphere where you can experience God and deepen your walk with Him!

Stewarding Time
Intimacy with God

*T*here never seems like there is enough time in a day to get everything done that needs to be done, let alone the things that you *want* to get done! The story seems to replay itself over and over again, like a nightmarish version of Groundhog's Day. We wake up, go to work/school, come home, eat dinner, then go to bed. Repeat that over and over for 5-7 days a week, and you have lived the robotic life of most Americans.

If you add the demand of relationships to the day, such as a spouse, children, or even friends, then the day fills up even more, and you feel like a debtor to time itself. Between spending quality time with loved ones and the responsibilities that may come with having loved ones, on top of the regular daily grind, how can you find a decent amount of time to spend with God? It is impossible!

But what if I told you that there is a way to change the crazy? What if instead of you being a slave to your time, you were able to make your time serve you? Sounds pretty good, right?

The secret is called *stewardship*. While this word applies to many areas of your life—including finances, responsibilities, relationships, etc.—it has the potential to change your daily existence completely!

Here's the thing—time is not fluid. You never have more or less of it in a day. Time is constant. Every single day you will have precisely 24 hours before the next day begins. What *is* fluid is how you steward the time you have in a day.

The reality is this: You have all the time you need in a day to do everything you want. And that includes spending time with the Father. The question you have to ask yourself?

How bad do you want it?

Here are some practical ways to spend time with God:
- Limit your time on social media.
- Go to bed earlier to get more time at the start of the next day.
- Wake up earlier to get more uninterrupted time at the beginning of the day.
- Eliminate an extra-curricular activity that is taking up too much time.
- Set a schedule that you can stick to for a day, making sure to slot out times to seek God.
- Redeem dead time—use time in waiting rooms, traffic, etc. to pray and worship or read your Bible.
- "Practice the Presence"—train yourself to continually be thinking about God and His Kingdom so you can be in communion with Him the moment when you are not engaged in work, study, conversation, etc. Become more aware of His abiding presence.

- Set time apart as a family to do devotions, worship, and prayer.
- Get an audio Bible and listen to it on your commute to work.

Action Steps

1. Spend 5 minutes during your prayer time with God and ask Him to reveal areas of your daily life that are "time-thieves," robbing your time from God.

2. Make a plan to limit or eliminate those areas and do it as soon as possible.

Week 1 - Day 2
Practicing the Presence
Intimacy with God

*T*here was a man who lived during the 17th century by the name of Brother Lawrence. Brother Lawrence was a lay monk in a Carmelite monastery in Paris. He served and worked in this monastery, devoting his life to the service of God.

That service included work such as cleaning dishes, pots, and pans, as well as cleaning floors and other tasks of the like.

Brother Lawrence of the Resurrection (as he was known) is best remembered by Christian history for the intimacy with God that he would often express he possessed. But this was no pious or self-righteous claim—this was the truth!

So true, in fact, that people traveled from near and far to watch him clean the monastery floors and dishes! I don't know about you, but that seems strange to me. I hate looking at the pile of dishes that inevitably awaits my arrival at the end of each day. With my family of eight, dirty dishes become the stuff of nightmares!

So what about Brother Lawrence caused people to travel from

all over to see him serve in these menial tasks?

It was his intimacy with the Lord that was at work and tangible while he performed these menial tasks. This level of intimacy with God during the mundane moments of life is referred to as "practicing the presence of God." His writings concerning this subject, as well as the story of his ministry, were compiled into a book called *Practicing the Presence of God.*

This practice is one of those things in Christianity that if you caught it, it would transform your relationship with God, which then, in turn, will change your life!

The essence of this practice is this: I am consciously going to increase my awareness of God's omni-presence (His always present presence). Everything I do will be "as for the Lord" (Colossians 3:23, ESV) as I live in constant communion with Him.

Brother Lawrence did this with every task he set his hands to at the monastery. As a result, the presence of God was so tangible that it drew crowds of people who longed to experience God in such a way in their own lives.

When I was home during the summer leading into my sophomore year of college, I had a painting job. We worked at these incredible mansions just doing outdoor maintenance on their buildings. This summer, we were working on one gigantic mansion that required me to spend full days on 48-foot ladders—nothing but me, the paint, and my thoughts. So I began to talk to God. I started to pour out my heart, spend time in silence as I lost myself in the task, and listening carefully for the voice of God. That summer taught me a lot about living in continual communion with God!

Action Steps

1. To warm up into this, determine checkpoints during your day to pause and turn your attention to God (maybe you want to pause at the top of each hour, every 30 minutes, good natural breaks in the work hours, etc.).

2. Communion with God is learning how to live in a relationship where you are consistently conscious of His presence. And every relationship is two-way. A lot of this is learning how to focus while listening to God. During checkpoints, or even as you go about your day, have moments of intentional quietness and openness to God and start looking/listening for what He wants to communicate to you.

Week 1 - Day 3
The Place of Rest
Intimacy with God

*I*t is no secret that we live in a world where our days are consumed with busyness (especially in our American culture). Wake up, go to work, have meetings, make phone calls, deal with people issues, deal with traffic, get home, make time for family and friends, find time for extra commitments and events, eat dinner, go to sleep, repeat. The busyness is not just a time-stewardship issue, but also a spiritual-rest issue.

Rest is a huge part of living a lifestyle of prayer and communion with the presence of God. Living from the place or state of rest is tied so closely with yesterday's devotional on *Practicing the Presence*. It is a state of inward spiritual rest that is the fruit of consistent awareness of the presence of God. It does not matter what is happening around you—war, strife, anxiety, economic turmoil, uncertainty, fear, accusations, attacks, persecution, etc.—because you have peace in your connection to God.

There is an account of a run-in Jesus and His disciples have with the Pharisees on a Sabbath recorded in Mark 2. Jesus and the disciples are walking through a grain field, and the disciples are hungry, so they begin to pluck the heads off the grain and crush them in their hands to eat. This would have been considered a big no-no to the Pharisees and their interpretation of the Law of Moses that governed Jewish daily life. So, naturally, they question Jesus about His disciples.

Jesus' response is nothing short of incredible.

> *"The Sabbath was made for man, not man for the Sabbath. So the Son of Man is lord even of the Sabbath."*[7]

I don't know what your background was like, but I grew up in the Church. And for as long as I can remember, there has always been a high importance placed on the Sabbath. Some families that I knew did not allow their kids to do any extra activities on Sundays. Others took the approach that it was important to have a "Sabbath day" somewhere in the week. However, having a day of physical rest does not come close to the purpose of the Sabbath.

When we take the idea of Sabbath and make it a rule we must observe, we fall into the last category of Jesus' statement, living as though we were made for the Sabbath. But Jesus says the opposite is true—the Sabbath (literally translates to mean "rest") was made for man. Rest is the product of our pursuit of God. When we seek to increase our awareness of His ever-abiding Presence, we find it in the stillness of mind and heart. We find it in the place of rest. It is where we find our rich and deep communion with God.

Why were the disciples terrified in the storm while Jesus slept? Jesus lived in the place of rest. How were the disciples able to do what

---

7 Mark 2:27-28

was seemingly illegal according to the Law and yet be innocent? They understood Jesus was the Lord of the Sabbath, and they were learning to live in this place of rest. Why were Christians in the Early Church able to sing songs of praise to God as they were being crucified and burned alive? They found the place of rest.

Action Steps

1. Take a moment and close your eyes. Put out all of the stress, frustration, and busy thoughts. Empty yourself before God and ask Him to help you live from that place of rest.

2. Continue to practice the presence and steadily increase your awareness of His presence every day.

3. Take time each day—especially when the craziness starts to take over—and "step away" from the moment and ask God for His perspective. Ask to see what He is doing.

4. Think back on moments of high stress in your life and give it some critical thinking. Look to see what God was doing, speaking, leading, or teaching you during those times.

5. When life gets overwhelming, remember the place of rest and turn your focus immediately back to God.

Week 1 - Day 4
Pursuit
Intimacy with God (Darcie)

"One thing have I asked of the Lord, that will I seek after: that I may dwell in the house of the Lord all the days of my life, to gaze upon the beauty of the Lord and to inquire in His temple." (Psalm 27:4)

This psalm was written by King David early on in his life when he was not yet king. In fact, not only was he not the king of Israel, but he had been betrayed and was being hunted down by his father-in-law, Saul, who was the king of Israel.

While on the run, you would think that David's chief concern would be safety! You would think that the psalm should read like this: "One thing have I asked of the Lord, that will I seek after: that I may be saved from Saul."

But David does not write that. He may be concerned with his safety and the safety of the men who were loyal to him, but that is not what consumes his thoughts and drives his steps. His greatest, motivating desire is that he would be in the presence of God! His current path was fleeing from King Saul, but that journey would eventually come to an end one way or another. His pursuit of God's presence, on the other hand, would never end!

The pursuit of God is a life-long journey that is never finished. Some stop and think that they have "arrived"—that there is no need to grow spiritually anymore or push any deeper into God's presence and love. They believe that they have reached the culmination of their relationship with Him.

At the same time, we believe that God is infinite and immeasurable. That means that there is no end to the depth of God to explore, discover, and experience. How sad it is for those who have accepted their current level of growth as "good enough!"

I find that those who so quickly stop growing in intimacy with the Lord do so because they have a poor understanding of this journey. They think it is one-sided. They believe that God is stationary and that they are the only ones doing the pursuing. How sad is this thinking?

The fact of the matter is that God is eagerly pursuing you! Take a look at Psalm 23:6,

> "Surely your goodness and love will follow me all the days of my life, and I will dwell in the house of the Lord forever."

That word, "follow," in the original Hebrew language is a military term. It gives the picture of a military force pursuing an enemy until it overtakes and overwhelms that enemy.

Do you understand what this verse means? The goodness and lovingkindness of God are eagerly pursuing us until they overtake us! God will never stop pursuing us until He overtakes us and overwhelms us with His goodness and love. He is not satisfied with where you currently are in your walk with Him. He wants to take you deeper. And as you pursue deeper wells of intimacy with Him, He pursues you with great passion!

Notice the second half of this verse. Once God overtakes us, it is then—at that point—that we dwell in the presence of God forever. David found his singular and greatest desire (which must be ours as well) as He pursued his God who was pursuing him!

God is not hard to find. EJ always says, "God is the worst at playing hide-and-seek!" And how true that is! He is not some far off, distant being that we have to struggle to find. He *wants* to be found by you. He *longs* to be found by you!

What would happen if you became dissatisfied with where you are in your relationship with God and decided to pursue Him passionately? The possibilities and experiences are endless!

Action Steps

1. Take a few moments today to think about your top 5 greatest desires that you have been taking steps in pursuit of in your life. If God is not one of them, take some time to ask yourself why?

2. Evaluate the condition of your relationship with God. Are you moving forward and deeper? Have you taken a few steps backwards? Are you stagnant and apathetic? No matter where you are in your relationship with God, you can always go deeper. Take a few minutes in prayer to ask God to reveal to

you His pursuit of you.

3. Once you get a glimpse of God's passionate pursuit after you, begin to express your love and gratitude to Him. Ask Him to take you deeper into His presence and to greater depths of intimacy than you have been before. Then let Him go to work on you as you wait on Him in silence.

Identity
Intimacy with God

$\mathcal{L}$et's be honest with ourselves for a few moments. Mankind is messed up! We are a people with such diverse opinions, mindsets, emotions, and world views. We are always dealing with some issue or obstacle in our lives. And those issues or obstacles affect us significantly—changing us and molding us even at times. They affect how we think, how we treat others, the decisions we make, how we react in certain situations, and so on.

I once was on the streets of Norwich, Connecticut, just showing the love of Jesus to people and talking about how much God cared for them as opportunities to engage in conversation arose.

One moment sticks out above the rest. We were taking shelter from the bitter cold bite of the winter wind inside of a gas station. A Muslim man was working as the cashier and began engaging one of my friends about Christianity, completely unprompted. While this conversation was happening, I briefly walked outside and crossed paths with two young adult women who were walking by. Again, unprompted, they asked us what we were all doing. So I told them we are just talking about God and Jesus.

Her reaction broke my heart. She said, "I hate God and Jesus," and then turned around and walked off with her friend. I wasn't satisfied with that being the end of our conversation. I called out after her, "Why do you hate Him?" She shouted back, "He took my father away from me!" And that was the last I saw of her.

The experiences we go through in life can shape us and mold us into who we are today.

What you need to understand, however, is that almost every time, those experiences that shape us produce a version of us that we were not created to be! Without a relationship with God to guide us through our experiences, our true identity becomes twisted into a counterfeit version of that identity. And that counterfeit is a lie from the enemy that we so easily buy into and allow to dictate how we think, believe, and act.

So what is your true identity? I am so glad that you asked!

> *"But when the fullness of time had come, God sent forth his Son, born of woman, born under the Law, to redeem those who were under the Law, so that we might receive adoption as sons."*[8]

There it is! You are sons (and daughters) of God! This idea of sonship communicated more in the culture of Jesus' day than it does in our day (which I write more about and about the subject of true identity in my book, *Sons of Liberty*). What this verse means is that it does not matter what your gender, ethnicity, background, culture,

---

8 Galatians 4:4-5

or country of residence is—you are a beloved child of God. And as a child of God, you have all the rights, authority, and responsibility that comes with that status. But the most significant benefit of this fact is the healing of your identity. Once you catch this and begin to believe it and grow in it, you finally start to see who God created you to be! All the junk that our counterfeit personality produced begins to disappear as we step into our true identities.

So don't settle for who you believe you are today. Allow God to come and renew your mind so that you see who He made you to be. Let Him take away the damage of all those experiences that have shaped you negatively through the years (whether you noticed their effects or not).

Become who you were born to be.

Become who He created you to be.

Live as the child of God that you are!

Action Steps

1. Read John 1:12; Romans 8:14-16; Galatians 3:26; Galatians 4:1-7.

2. Make a list of all the experiences in your life that negatively impacted you or changed how you thought.

3. Take a few moments to ask God to reveal to you the effects of experiences that you were not aware of that negatively affected your identity. Combine the two lists.

4. Pray over this combined list one by one and ask God to remove them and heal you from their effects. Then take the verses above and speak them over each of the points on your list, using the verses as a reason why those points are not true of who you are.

5. Whenever you face a situation that threatens to affect how you view yourself, remind yourself of these verses.

Burying the Orphan Heart
Intimacy With God

*T*here is a verse in the Bible that is fascinating, yet alarming if we do not consider its implications. It is found in John 14:18,

> *"'I will not leave you as orphans; I will come to you.'"*

This is part of Jesus' response to Philip when he asks Jesus to show them God, the Father. The truth of this verse is fascinating in that it is calling those who are without the Father orphans. The implication is that before your relationship with God, which provides your identity as "sons," you were a spiritual orphan.

However, just because an adoption takes place, and the orphan is living in a home with a family, does not necessarily mean that their identity and mindset have changed. They may no longer be an orphan in status, but they may continue to feel like an orphan in their heart.

This mentality is often referred to as the orphan heart. It is a spiritual attack upon our identity as God's children, trying to hinder us from ever fully walking into what God has planned for us. That fullness of life can only be accessed by walking in our true identity.

This orphan spirit has many symptoms that can be seen in others (even in ourselves) daily.

The following is a few examples of the symptoms of spiritual orphans taken directly from Jack Frost's book, *Spiritual Slaves to Spiritual Sons*:

- "Orphans see God as a master they must appease continually...Sons, on the other hand, see God as a loving Father who accepts them unconditionally."
- "Orphans generally possess a low self-image and an attitude of self-rejection, which results from comparing themselves to others and feeling that they come out on the short end of the stick...Sons feel positive and affirmed because they know how valuable and precious they are to their Father. No matter what they do or how many times they mess up, they know that Father loves them anyway."
- "Orphans...generally resort to accusation and exposure of other people's faults—while denying or trying to hide their own...Sons are relationship-oriented. In love, they cover (not hide) others' faults as they seek to restore those individuals in a spirit of love and gentleness."
- "Orphans are guarded and conditional in their expression of love. Expressed love by an orphan is based on others' performance and agreement...For sons, love is open, transparent, and affectionate. They lay down their own agendas in order to meet the needs of others."

These are just a few of the many differences between a spiritual orphan and a spiritual son. I hope you see that living far from sonship—the Bible's term for living as a mature child of God—is detrimental to living an incredible life on Earth.

The whole Bible communicates the message that God was drawing us back to Him—reconciling us back to Him. He longs for us to experience what life can really be like! And a life of prayer and practicing the presence is essential to healing the orphan heart and keeping the wound closed forever.

Action Steps

Answer the following statements, ranking them 1-5
(1 = Never | 5 = Regularly)

1. I see God as the one who punishes me when I sin.

   1   2   3   4   5

2. I feel that I am not as important to God as others around me.

   1   2   3   4   5

3. I need affirmation from others to feel any value.

   1   2   3   4   5

4. I am constantly comparing myself to other people.

1   2   3   4   5

5. I struggle to pray because I get stuck in sin so often.

1   2   3   4   5

6. My friendships typically last as long as they make me feel good.

1   2   3   4   5

7. I have to try my hardest to be a good person for God to be pleased.

1   2   3   4   5

If you answered any of the above statements with anything but a #1 (never), then the orphan heart is trying to take control. Spend some time on these statements in prayer and ask God to deal with them and give you a heart of sonship instead.

Week 1 - Day 7
The Gaze of the Heart
Intimacy with God

$\mathcal{B}$ill Johnson, lead pastor of Bethel Church in Redding, California, has been quoted saying, "You are what you behold." I find this to be true in my own life and the lives of others. What I fix my attention upon regularly often has a heavy influence on my life.

If my thoughts and attention are consistently upon another woman and not my wife, my marriage will suffer, if not completely fail due to an act of infidelity. If I have an unprovoked altercation with someone in a store, and I allow myself to watch the instant replay in my mind over and over again, my attitude will be negative about other things throughout the day. Likewise, when I spend all my time with negative or critical people, I find myself becoming more and more negative and critical.

When we are talking about intimacy with God—having a deeper, meaningful relationship with Him—the focus of our heart's affection is crucial!

The late Chicago-based pastor/author A.W. Tozer referred to

this focus as the "gaze of the heart." He taught that this relationship with God, and our faith in Him, is not a singular act or momentary commitment. It is a continual gaze of the heart upon God. It is about fixing our attention upon Him above all other things that can distract us. He wants your attention! God does not play second-fiddle to anyone. No friend settles for shallow interactions. No spouse will accept half-hearted devotion. No meaningful relationship survives on limited affection. God wants the focus of our heart's eye to be fixated on Him. God is not some egotistical being that needs our affection. He doesn't need our love. He wants our *willing* love! And He has extended Himself and lavished His love upon each of us, hoping we will reciprocate.

You must understand, however, that the love He gave was not for His benefit but our own. When the gaze of our heart is fixed on Him, the way we live our life radically changes!

A follower of Jesus who lives with their heart's gaze on Jesus has the incredible ability to stop in the middle of their day, regardless of what going on around them, close their eyes, and instantly find themselves in the sweet presence of their Father. In that place, they find the love, acceptance, peace, strength, and joy that they need to respond to whatever they may be facing that day.

This is love. This is experiencing the depths of God. This is understanding who you really are. This is walking as a true child of God.

This is intimacy with God.

Action Steps

1. Come up with a way to remind yourself at different check-points throughout your day to pause and practice realigning the gaze of your heart upon God.

2. In those moments, simply ask God to make you the object of His affection. Then sit in the stillness and allow God to move.

Week 2 - Day 1
Relationships
Practice of Prayer

*G*od is the creator of relationships. He exists Himself within the relationship between the Father, Son, and Holy Spirit. And one of the most important relationship systems that God has created is that of the family.

Family is extremely important to God. This type of relationship was given by God to reveal the framework of God's Kingdom to mankind. Heaven is pictured as a wedding feast—the joining of families. The Church is viewed as the Bride of Christ. The apostles in the Early Church referred to the individual members of the Church as brothers and sisters. The relationship between God and Man is described by scripture as a marriage. The governmental structure within the Church is intended to be based on love and submission to authority. Paul referred to the younger men he invested as his "sons," and the people in the churches he served as his "children."

Paul addresses the book of Philemon to a man named Philemon, whose servant ran away to Paul. Paul writes to Philemon to tell him to accept this servant openly and to treat him like a member of his family.

God places such a high importance on family that He sent His only Son to be born into a family, at a time when everyone had to return by law to the town of their family's origin. God sends Jesus into the world into the arms of a mother and father, who are surrounded by extended family (since Joseph's family was from Bethlehem).

If the idea of family is so important to God, then there is great need to place high importance on the condition of our own physical families. But if you look around in our culture today (especially in the United States), it seems as if the model of family has been thrown out and replaced with all kinds of imposters: divorced parents, single mothers, single fathers, runaway kids, widows, orphans, homosexual homes, abusive homes, alcoholic homes, homes full of drug addicts, illegitimate children, etc.

The enemy has been hard at work, trying to dismantle the family unit. He wants nothing more than to see finances, deceit, defiance, lust, disrespect, rebellion, bitterness, apathy, anger, and the like to find a footing and tear the family to shreds.

We must commit ourselves to protect our own families at all costs. We must not allow the traps of the enemy to find their way into our homes!

If your family is facing relational struggles, whether your immediate family or extended family, I have one question for you: What are you going to do about it? Seriously! How are you going to bring healing and wholeness to this part of the family so that the presence of God can flow, and everyone can walk in who they were created to be?

Action Steps – 1/2

1. Make a list of the family members who are far from God, those you have broken relationships with, or those whith whom your relationship is strained.

2. Pray about how God wants to bring reconciliation to the broken or strained relationships. Then next to or below those names, write down intentional ways to restore those relationships. Pray for opportunities to reconcile with them.

3. Write the names of your family members who are far from God on a few notecards and keep them somewhere.

Action Steps – 2/2

1. If you have strong, healthy relationships, then create a list of the top 5 important relationships in your life.

2. Next to or below this list, pray about and write down ways to strengthen these relationships.

Fasting

Practice of Prayer

*F*asting is one of those spiritual disciplines that is difficult to get people excited about. The idea of withholding food from yourself sounds like a horrible, unattractive diet and not a way to grow in your relationship with the Lord or bring depth to your prayer life.

No matter how you feel about fasting, it is essential to the life of the believer. It is one of three disciplines that Jesus says are "givens" in the life of one of His followers.

> *"'...When you give...and when you pray...and when you fast...'"*[9]

These are not helpful suggestions to the life of a Christian. These are essential! What sets the practice of fasting apart from the rest is the dependency it fosters upon the Spirit of God. As you fast from food, you are weakening your body to a degree, which then

---

9 Matthew 6:3, 5, 16

makes you more aware of your weaknesses and limitations. As you focus your attention on God and become less dependent upon the food for strength, you will find that your strength becomes more dependent on God. It is important to note that fasting must be done within safe health practices and sometimes even in consultation with your doctor, especially if you already have health issues.

When done properly and safely, fasting will make you more sensitive and focused on God than you are in the typical "hustle and bustle" of your day.

There are different kinds of fasts that we see in the Bible (Various types of fasts, their purposes, and their scripture references are located in the back of the book in the *Resources* section). There are also various purposes, goals, and occasions for fasting. But regardless of all those specific details, there is a single goal above the rest: to know God more.

Many people think about fasting when there are issues or questions in their lives that they are facing. And these are great times to fast, no doubt. But if that is the only time you are fasting, then you have missed the mark entirely. All that communicates is that you are fasting because of the enemy. We do not fast to square off with the devil. We fast to get closer to God so that when those issues and attacks come, we are already prepared to handle them.

This life of prayer, including fasting, is all about drawing ever nearer to God. Don't settle for your current depth of relationship with God right now. He is infinite! That means that there is always more of God to have!

To find out more details on some of the primary fasts we see in the Bible, check out the list provided in the back of the book in the Tools for Developing Spiritual Maturity section.

Action Steps

1. Choose a fast that you feel confident about doing from the list in the back of this book. Set a date on your calendar for the fast to begin.

2. When choosing a day, make sure it is one that you can devote your attention to seeking God. If you do it on a big event day or a day filled with activities you are not going to be fasting; you will only be skipping meals.

Revelation
Practice of Prayer

*O*ften during prayer, God is looking to communicate with you. Sometimes it is an impression or a quiet small voice on the inside. Other times it is dreams, waking-dreams, visions, images, or random thoughts He drops in your mind. You see, God's language is not like our own. It is far more complex and varied and goes way beyond mere words. Sometimes He speaks through a lyric in a song. Other times His voice is heard through the sunrise or sunset. He may use the words of others to speak, the words read on a page, or through the thunder over the ocean.

God is always speaking to us. And there are special times when He speaks to us intending to reveal truth to us. That type of communication is what we call "revelation".

Revelation from God can be a moment of clarity in a difficult situation. It can be a verse in the Bible that you've read over and over before, but now jumps out at you and grips your attention. Revelation can be a dream at night or a vision during the day that God gives you.

During prayer and resting in His Presence, the Lord may give you revelation by impressing images or thoughts upon your mind.

No matter how God gives us revelation, we must receive it well. What is the point of wisdom if we do not apply it to our lives? The same is true of revelation. If we receive it, or worse, experience it but do not recognize it, and fail to apply that revelation to our lives, we have effectively shut the door on what God was trying to do.

Sometimes when revelation is given, it is meant to be kept to yourself. The Bible records that Mary, the mother of Jesus, hid in her heart all of the prophecies and revelation about Jesus—decades before He ever walked in the fullness of those prophecies.

Whether revelation comes to accomplish something in your present or in your future, the point is that revelation comes to accomplish something.

So as you continue to seek God this week, pay attention to the random and odd thoughts that you would typically write off. Keep a sharp eye out for what God may be trying to do. Listen carefully for His voice in the many places it may echo.

Action Steps

1. Buy a journal and keep it with a pen by your bed. If you have a dream that you feel may be from God, no matter how weird—write it down with as much detail as possible.

2. If God gives you dreams of visions, ask Him to show you what they mean.

3. If you feel a verse jump out at you as you read the Bible, make a note of it. Don't continue you day and forget about it. Think upon it throughout your day. Mull it over and ask God what it is He is trying to speak to you.

4. If you understand what God is speaking to you…apply it!

5. When you wake up, ask God to speak to you that day. When you go to sleep, ask God to speak to you that night. Do this every day this week and record what happens.

Praying for Enemies
Practice of Prayer

*L*et's face t. Sometimes Jesus said some things that are hard to swallow. Probably chief among them is when He made the statement,

> *"But I tell you, love your enemies and pray for those who persecute you."*[10]

It seems to me that there were so many other steps that could have been taken before jumping right to loving our enemies and praying for them. He jumped right to the extreme. He did this to challenge the self-righteous, imperfect interpretations of the religious teachers that taught, "An eye for an eye." If someone wrongs you, you have the right to seek retribution.

However, Jesus says the opposite is true. If someone wrongs you, you must release that offense and return offense with love and prayer.

---

10 Matthew 5:44

This teaching of Jesus is part of what we call the Sermon on the Mount—a lengthy and detailed discourse on what it means to live in His Kingdom while on Earth. Prayer is, at its core, essentially an intentional move away from the thoughts, patterns, and ways of this world, and the intentional movement towards the thoughts, patterns, and ways of the Kingdom of God. When we pray, we are either pushing earthly things away to immerse ourselves into the culture of Heaven, or grabbing hold of the culture of Heaven and releasing it on Earth.

So how do you move past the thoughts and opinions and facts that label a person your enemy? How do you remove the memories of pain enough to be able to pray for that person with sincerity?

The answer is that we must see them as the person that God had originally created them to be. Nobody is born evil or cruel. In fact, the Bible speaks to just the opposite. God created everything good! The problem is that sin has twisted people far from the image of God that they were originally intended to be. In turn, they treat others from the twisted nature and through their words and actions begin twisting and affecting the image of others, which produces more people who become enemies of others. It is a vicious cycle.

But we are called to end that vicious cycle through love and prayer. The love of God enables us to love our enemies with His love—*unconditional* love. This love removes any inkling that the other person must earn your love through works and replaces it with a love that is not dependent on how they treat you. Prayer, as part of the answer, enables you to see Kingdom transformation invade their lives.

Because at the end of the day, your "enemy" is a child of God who is struggling to know they have a Father in Heaven who loves them and is with them.

I cannot think of anyone more deserving of our love and

prayers!

Action Steps

1. Pull out a calendar (paper, phone app, etc.) and assign one person who could be labeled an "enemy" in your life to each of the following three weeks.

2. Read Matthew chapters 26-27. Before reading, ask God to show you the intensity of what Jesus went through and to help you understand His great love for all mankind.

3. Pray for these "enemies." Ask God to show you the reasons why they behave the way they do towards you and that He would fill you with compassion for them to pray effectively.

Week 2 - Day 5
Worship
Practice of Prayer

*W*orship and prayer are uniquely intertwined when it comes to a lifestyle of prayer. They cannot be separated, or else they are each incomplete. They can exist separate from each other, but the life of prayer is most effective and impactful when they are working in conjunction with one another. They are two sides of the same coin.

Worship increases our awareness of God's Presence, which then enables prayer to push into that presence through intimate communion. No intentional prayer time should exclude some facet of worship.

Worship has been a concept that has been around for millennia. Most cultures throughout history have chosen to worship some idea of a being. But the idea of what worship is has taken on many forms. The Bible records how some nations worshipped: sacrificing animals, sacrificing children, singing songs, playing music, cutting themselves, dancing around, chanting, etc.

We believe that there is only one God. So the question of the day is this: what is the kind of worship that pleases Him?

Worship is much more than singing a song. It is much more than 20-30 minutes of music during a church service. These things are all merely tools that help facilitate worship but are not worship in and of themselves.

Worship is the expression of the heart to communicate the love, awe, gratefulness, and wonder we have towards our heavenly Father. When we make this idea of worship part of our lifestyle, we will find that our connection to God and sensitivity to His presence and voice will be deeper and clearer. From there, we can communicate with God and pray on a whole different level—one in which we have the heart and mind of God, which makes prayer and intercession far more effective because we are tapping into the very will of God Himself!

Action Steps

1. "Tools" are not wrong to use to aid in our worship (worship playlists, etc.) They are very helpful! From now on, portion aside part of your private time with the Lord for worship.

2. Make a list of 50 things you are thankful to God for and then express the thankfulness for those things one by one down the list.

Persevering Prayer
Practice of Prayer

*E*very believer at one time or another has felt that their prayers have gone unanswered. While I believe that sometimes this is because we are praying according to our will instead of God's will, I also believe that there are times when we stop praying too soon. I am not merely talking about the length of our prayers, but the perseverance of our prayers.

1 Kings 18 is a fascinating chapter in the Bible. The prophet Elijah was one of the last remnant of Israelites still serving God. The wicked King Ahab—who married the idolatrous and infamous Jezebel—had led all of Israel away from the Lord and ensnared them with idol worship. Ahab and Jezebel hated Elijah. He spoke out against their rule and their character qualities, and he even prophesied that rain would not fall in Israel as a challenge to their beloved storm-god, Baal. No matter what they did, it seemed as if Ahab and Jezebel would never come close to stopping Elijah.

After an incredible showdown on Mt. Carmel—where God

proved Himself to be the one true God and Baal to be false, leading Israel back into worship of their true God—Elijah goes back up to the top of Mt. Carmel to pray for rain and tells his servant to get a view of the sea to see if rain was coming.

This part of the story is where things get interesting! The first time the servant went looking for the answer to Elijah's prayers, he saw nothing. He also saw nothing the second time. And the third, fourth, fifth, and sixth times. Only on the seventh time that Elijah sent him did the servant see anything remotely resembling an answer to the prayer.

> *"Behold, a little cloud like a man's hand is rising from the sea."* [11]

I don't know about you, but my track record with this kind of persevering prayer has not been great in the past. In our American culture, we are used to fast and convenient results. We want what we want, and we want it now!

On which time that Elijah sent his servant to view the sea did the servant begin thinking, "I don't know if Elijah is right on this one. It's not looking too good right now. I don't think God is going to do what Elijah is saying He will do."

But sure enough, on the seventh time he went, the servant sees a small, barely-qualified-to-be-mentioned cloud.

Now to most of us, this would not be proof enough to encourage us that God is answering our prayers. We could quickly write this off as random. But Elijah does the exact opposite. He hears the news and sends his servant off to deliver the news to King Ahab. And when

---

11 1 Kings 18:44 (ESV)

this servant left, Elijah did not get up satisfied that God would complete what He started, but rather continued to pray until the prayer was fully answered.

> *"And in a little while the heavens grew black with clouds and wind, and there was a great rain."* [12]

There are times when we can know the will of God in a situation just by knowing His character. That knowledge can lead us to pray with confidence for His will to be done. But sometimes, we must contend in prayer—do some warfare intercession—and persevere in our prayers. There are times when a simple or even an elaborate prayer falls short. When God leads you to pray over specific things, there are moments when you must pray through to the answer.

Don't get up and be discouraged after a few prayers and what seems like no response. Do not get up once you think you see a potential answer. Stay in the posture of prayer until the rain is pouring down, and you feel it on your head. God is a good Father and desires to honor and bless His children. Jesus told us to ask, and what we ask for would be given to us. God wants to answer our prayers, but how many times do we give up too soon when we were just about to see the wisps of the cloud forming?

Action Steps

1. Identify the one or two significant prayers that you have

---

12 1 Kings 18:45 (ESV)

prayed for that have not yet been answered.

2. Spend some time in self-reflection, asking, "Is it my will or God's will that fuels this prayer?" If it is your will, ask God to come and renew your mind to see His will in the situation. If it is God's will that motivates you, then press on and persevere.

3. Read the stories of others in the Bible who had to persevere in prayer: Daniel (21 days), Jesus (40 days), and the apostles (the time between Christ's resurrection and Pentecost), to name a few.

Week 2 - Day 7
Identification in Intercession
The Practice of Prayer (Darcie)

*W*hen you were younger, you probably heard the Golden Rule: "Do to others as you would have them do to you." It is something that all of us still need to understand and practice. I find myself saying this to my children often! "How would you like it if…" Or "Wouldn't you like it if someone shared with you?" We have heard these words since childhood, yet we still struggle with putting others before ourselves. Our culture teaches us to think about ourselves at any cost. But the Bible teaches us something completely different. The Bible teaches us to die to self—the very thing Jesus did for us. Philippians 2:6-8 states,

> *"Who (Jesus) being in very nature God, did not consider equality with God something to be grasped, but made himself nothing, taking the very nature of a servant, being made in human likeness. And being found in appearance as a man, he humbled himself and became obedient to death—even death on a cross!"*

How would our prayer life change if we practiced "doing to others as we would want them to do to us"? What if we prayed with the same intensity if it was our need? Our family? Our job on the line? I think we would see the Church come alive in a new way! When we practice empathy and compassion, we can shift the atmosphere in our prayer life!

Since I was a young girl, I always wanted to be a mother. I would play "house" daily. I would have fake weddings, dedicate my baby dolls to the Lord, and even had a "mom" birthday party when I was around 5! As I grew up, my passion for motherhood remained strong. When EJ and I were courting, we felt that God called us to trust Him in when to have kids, and to trust Him with how many He would decide to give us. Little did I know that we would be a full tribe of 5 children in a matter of 8 years!

But what if He didn't give us children? How would I have felt? The truth is, I have had countless friends unable to have children. I started to feel awkward. I felt a burden for these friends. Should I not talk to them about my children? Should I ask them to pray for them? What if God doesn't answer that prayer? I have had many phone conversations and altar experiences, where I have cried with my friends who were not seeing a fulfillment of their dreams come true, all the while when I continue to have baby after baby.

It was during the season of life when sleep was nonexistent that God shifted my prayer life. With every spiritual gift test I took, intercession was always on the low end. I thought I was good at praying for people, but I was never passionate about interceding for others. I asked God to change that. I wanted to pray for others in the same way that I hope others would pray for me. This kind of prayer is

51

called "identification in intercession." One of the nights I was up with a sweet but needy baby, God shifted my whole idea of prayer! I was crying, rocking this baby who needed to have some form of physical contact with me, and said, "God, I don't want to do this anymore!" I was sleep-deprived. I was angry. I just wanted to sleep like a teenager again. And that's when I felt the Holy Spirit say, "Why not use your time wisely?" I was too tired to read, as my own mother suggested. I didn't know how to use my time wisely. So I started to pray for whoever came to mind. It felt random. It felt weird! Some people I hadn't spoken to in a while. But I continued. I would pray for whatever I felt the Holy Spirit drop into my heart.

I started to share with some of these people what I felt to pray for them. And whoa! I didn't just learn to pray; I learned how to listen to the Holy Spirit and to obey. Once I realized the importance of these prayers, I started to pray harder. I would cry as if it were my marriage, my children, my womb that I wanted God to be open. I would pray for destiny, purpose and fulfillment of promises. I would rock my sleepy baby and pray hard! I did not notice how time slipped away. I didn't even know then how praying affected my little boy, who is a prayer warrior himself now! I saw the blessings of my obedience come to pass. And I learned to be a prayer warrior for others.

I sit here smiling, remembering the testimonies of people whose lives were affected by my prayers. What a humbling thought! I think of the babies born and those still in the womb of my friends who are expecting. I think of how God took what I deemed a negative situation, and how He turned it into one of my most rewarding lessons ever learned. I am glad that I obeyed.

So I challenge you today, how do you pray? Do you pray for others the way you want them to pray for you? When a friend is sharing with you, stop at that moment and pray! Don't say, "I will keep you in prayer"; start right then and there! Let your prayers be effective! Let your prayers be the ones that are passionate and detailed. Be wise with your time. Pray in the shower. Pray in the car. Pray when you think of someone, and then call them. Be sensitive to the Holy Spirit. Pray when you're cooking dinner or when you are grocery shopping. Prayer time doesn't always have to look like a certain way!

Action Steps

1. Ask three people this week if there is anything you can pray about for them. Keep asking people until you get three specific answers.

2. As you are spending time with God and preparing to pray for their needs, think about what it would be like to go through what they are going through. Think of the implications in your own life those issues would cause.

3. Allow the Holy Spirit to break your heart for them and pray passionately and specifically.

4. Set a reminder on your phone or calendar to follow up with them in a week and see how they are. You might be surprised to find that your prayers were answered!

Week 3 - Day 1
Dreams
The Prophetic Life of Prayer

$\mathcal{O}$nce, when I was in college, I had a dream about being in my grandmother's PT Cruiser and was being driven to Jamaica by a female classmate of mine while I sat in the passenger seat. In this dream, there were things like a guy I knew from New York packing all my belongings for me, and a pair of nice sneakers that had the colors of the Jamaican flag on them.

I woke up that morning feeling very confused but amazed at how vivid this dream was. Like most people, I initially thought it was something I ate the night before (college food…never fails) or thought that it was just my mind running wild with everything going on at college.

This experience was my first encounter (that I can vividly remember) with prophetic dreams. As I thought on this dream throughout the days to come, I felt positive that this was a dream from God and not some random creation of my subconscious.

So I began to research and pray for what this dream could

mean. I felt confident that God was bringing me to Jamaica to do ministry, that my provision would come from people I knew in New York, and that everything would be taken care of for me. Additionally, on a "stab-in-the-dark," I told the female classmate about the dream and asked her to be open to what God wanted to do.

Soon after all of this, two friends who had graduated from my bible college contacted me. They were leading a mission trip to Jamaica and wanted me to act as a kind of facilitator with some other students at the school. One of those students happened to be the female student I had dreamt about going with me.

I had very few funds coming in from my fundraising efforts and the deadline was two days away. I needed $1,100 in *two* days! I woke up the next morning to several checks in my school mailbox from a Christian concert management company that covered most of the cost, as well as other checks that made up the difference. Every single check from New York, where I was from!

This dream, although initially strange to me, came to pass with such precision that I had no choice but to research and seek after this subject some more.

After some study and keeping a greater awareness when it came to God-thoughts and dreams, I learned that God is constantly speaking to us in these more abstract ways! While it is important to realize that not every dream is prophetic/from God (and we must use discernment and be careful to not over-spiritualize), dreams are one of the major avenues through which God speaks to us.

Not only are prophetic dreams biblical, but they are to be a normal part of the Christian life. God is trying to speak to us about our lives, the lives of others, and about certain situations. He wants to warn us, encourage us, confirm decisions for us, and give us wisdom for life. And sometimes He chooses to do this through dreams.

But does God wait for us to become aware of prophetic dreams or to be dream interpretation gurus? No! So ask yourself this question: What has God been speaking to me in my dreams that I have missed?

Action Steps

1. Buy a blank journal. Keep it with a pencil/pen by your bed. This is your "dream journal." When God gives you a dream, it is important to write down everything you can remember with great detail. This is beneficial for prayer and reflection later, as well as encouragement to your faith when you see the dream has been fulfilled! Put the date and time on the entry so you can keep track of your dream's timing.

2. When you go to bed, ask God to speak to you in your dreams. If you have one, write it down immediately—even if you wake up from it in the middle of the night.

3. One of the biggest dream-thieves is television/media before bed. The hour before bed is a crucial time. When we fill our minds and spirits with what entertainment feeds us, it can follow us to bed. That is why when we watch an intense show, our dreams can follow that genre or storyline to bed in our dreams. Try starting the process of calming down your mind and heart the hour before bed.

Impressions
The Prophetic Life of Prayer

I was in one of our Sunday night youth services. We had fun before service in our youth lounge, played some hysterical games, had an amazing time of worship, and I had just preached my guts out to these students. The altars were full of students who were genuinely seeking their Father in Heaven. After we (my youth leaders and I) spent time with each student and praying with them, I began walking around as I typically do, surveying the scene.

And that's when it happened. As I was looking around, I saw one new student standing with another friend in the second row of chairs to my right. As soon as I saw him, I felt a thought—an impression—strike me (quite randomly, to be honest). It was one word.

Suicide

I don't know where you fall on the "bold-ometer," but this is not typically my strength. I wrestled with approaching this student for what felt like a very long time. *How is he going to receive this? Is he going to be weirded out or offended? What if I completely miss it?!*

After pushing past all of these fear-fueled thoughts, I approached the student with as much confidence as I could muster. I told him what I felt the Lord spoke to me, including some other specific things I felt God was revealing to me as I spoke to him. When I finished, I asked the big question: "Does any of that make sense to you?"

His response was…underwhelming: "Not really," he said.

Embarrassment does not even come close to describing how I felt. I walked away, confused. I really thought I had heard clearly from God. What happened? How had I missed it *so* badly?

After service was over and everyone was at our cafe or the lounge and hanging out, one of my younger youth leaders (a former youth student), came to me and was talking about how he had a good conversation with the "new kid." He told me that after I talked with him, the new student confessed to this youth leader that he had been struggling with depression and a lot of thoughts about taking his own life.

I was so encouraged! I had not missed it! I had clearly heard God's voice about this student through these impressions.

I tell you all of that to say this: It is crucial for us as followers of Jesus to always practice having a continual awareness of God's presence and His voice. We can get so caught up in our schedules, busyness, agendas, thoughts, and desires that we miss entirely and can be totally unaware of moments of what God is speaking to us in specific moments.

There are people all around us daily whose lives are waiting to be transformed by the voice of God. Not just the people we know well—not just people who are acquaintances. But strangers as well. Think about how many people you pass by every day. God is speaking to His children about them all the time. Are you listening?

In John 10:27, Jesus says, "My sheep listen to my voice; I know them, and they follow me." Often in Jesus' day, multiple herds of sheep belonging to different shepherds would graze in the same fields. They would intermix and be impossible for a shepherd to separate. But the sheep were so accustomed to their shepherd, that when he called, the sheep came running and ended up separating themselves. Why? Because they knew their shepherd's voice. They could distinguish his voice from others because of their time spent with him, their nearness to him, and their familiarity with his voice.

The same is true about hearing from God. He speaks in many ways, one of which is the impressions. How familiar are you with His voice? Can you distinguish when He is speaking to you and when it is just you thinking? The truth is this—God is always speaking to His children. You do not have to be a super-saint to hear His voice. He is not waiting for you to reach a spiritual peak in your walk with Him for Him to start speaking to you. It all comes down to familiarity and sensitivity with His voice. And the only way to get more familiar and sensitive—to become more aware—is through cultivating a lifestyle of prayer.

Action Steps

1. Spend time in silence in your designated prayer time this week. That means finding the time where you can be alone and are not feeling rushed to get to the next thing on your schedule. If you are struggling to find the time when you can do this, you may need to reevaluate your schedule and

reprioritize.

2. Set aside all distractions—Put your phone on silent, go to a place by yourself where you can be alone, Find a quiet place, leave any device behind that will send you notifications that may become a distraction. You know what eats your time and attention. Eliminate those things.

3. Pay attention to the thoughts or images that come to you. Write them down if you need to help to remember. Ask God to help you understand what He's saying to you.

Speaking Life
The Prophetic Life of Prayer

"*S*ticks and stones may hurt my bones, but words will never hurt me!" This popular response to name-calling when we were young kids in elementary school was our go-to to stand up to the harsh words of others. It was a shield—a statement of defiance in the face of unkindness.

The problem is that this statement is one big lie. Because the reality is, words *really do* hurt us. They sometimes have a way of sticking with us for days, months, even years at a time. The more hurtful words spoken over us can affect us in such a way that they twist our identity, our thought processes, and even begin to define us.

The New Testament writer, James, writes in his epistle (letter) that bears his name,

> *"When we put bits into the mouths of horses to make them obey us, we can turn the whole animal. Or take ships as an example. Although they are so large and are driven by strong*

winds, they are steered by a very small rudder wherever the pilot wants to go. Likewise, the tongue is a small part of the body, but it makes great boasts..."[13]

James is trying to communicate the power contained within the words we all speak (especially those of us who would teach the Word). The words we speak have the power to influence the direction and outcome of situations and lives.

Seeing the importance of the words we speak, how often do we think about the impact that the words we are about to speak will have? Taking it a step further, how often do we think about the effect that the words of our prayers we are about to pray will have?

Proverbs gives us a key to understand the importance of our words, especially when it comes to the prophetic life of prayer:

"Death and life are in the power of the tongue…"[14]

There are only two kinds of impacts that our words will have: Life or death. In our culture and the world today, we are most accustomed with speaking death—New reports about how horrible things are in our world or government/culture, Expressing frustrations in inappropriate ways, harsh words towards those we are angry with, gossiping about those who offend us, slandering the reputations of others, etc. And when we pray, we can often be speaking death over ourselves/situations. We pray things like, "God, judge them for what they did to me…be my vengeance!" or "God if it's your will…" We give God our frustrations but live empty of hope that things will

---

13 James 3:3-5
14 Proverbs 18:21 (ESV)

change instead of asking for an end to the situations we face. We are very familiar with hearing others "speak death" and with "speaking death" ourselves.

What we are not familiar with is "speaking life." And when it comes to prayer, this is so important. We have a literal power in the words we speak to affect change—both spiritually and physically. When we pray for healing, we speak life to a person's body, because Jesus broke the curse of sin and death. When we are told in Scripture to encourage and edify the Body of Christ, we are speaking life. Comforting words to a person who is grieving, depressed, discouraged, or all of the above, can be life-changing. And when God stirs our spirits to pray over seemingly hopeless situations, we do not confess the hopelessness in our prayers, but rather pray from a place of deep faith, believing that God can bring life into any situation!

Everything we speak and pray should bring life. Encouragement, prayers, conversations, corrections—all of it should speak life into people. If it doesn't communicate or bring life, it is better left unsaid and not prayed.

Action Steps

1. Read over Proverbs 18:21 multiple times throughout each day. Think about it and about the words you have been speaking. Keep the verse fresh in your mind for the rest of the week.

2. Before you address a situation or begin praying, ask yourself

if what you are about to say will bring life or death.

3. As a follower of Jesus, we are called to speak life into the
    lives of others. Think about some of the people around you in
    everyday life. What are some intentional ways God can speak
    life through you into their lives?

Intercession
The Prophetic Life of Prayer

In 1722, Count Nikolaus von Zinzendorf—a German count and devout man of God—opened up His property to form a community of Christians who were being persecuted. They called it *Herrnhut*. Shortly after he did this, a Moravian man approached him about the persecution and exile the Moravian believers were facing from their country. By 1726, this community of Herrnhut grew to about 300 Moravians. They placed a high emphasis on community, prayer, and worship as they lived together with Count Zinzendorf and his family.

On August 13, 1727, during a special Communion service, the Holy Spirit came into that meeting place with power and filled all in attendance. So powerful was this experience that Count Zinzendorf recorded that they were "hardly knowing whether they belonged to Earth or had already gone to Heaven."

They were so impacted by this moment that a few days later—on August 27—24 men and 24 women committed to praying for 1 hour each day, calling it "hourly intercession." This resulted in a passion for missions, and they became known for sending out the most missionaries throughout the world in their day. There are even accounts of Moravian missionaries selling themselves into slavery to gain access to countries that were closed to Christianity!

What a legacy they leave behind for us! But I want you to notice that they committed themselves to not just prayer, but also intercession. While all intercession is prayer, not all prayer is intercession. There is a difference! Prayer is essentially communion with God. It is talking with Him, worshipping, listening to Him, pouring out affections upon each other, delighting in each other, and talking about your needs, hopes, dreams, concerns, and gratitude. Prayer is practicing the Presence of God.

Intercession is a branch off of this definition of prayer. Intercession's most basic and classic definition is: "One who stands in the gap for another." We have a vivid and perfect picture of this in the person of Aaron, Moses' brother —the first High Priest of the Old Testament. In Numbers 16, the Israelites invite a plague upon themselves through their sinful actions. As the plague was breaking out all over the entire nation of Israelites gathered, God commands Aaron to take his censer (bowl) with incense burning in it (representing prayer & intercession) and run into the midst of the people. He literally stood in the gap between the dead and the living. As a result, the plague immediately stopped!

That is the perfect picture of what an intercessor does. They stand in the gap, through prayer, for others. They do battle in the spirit for the sake of other people, communities, families, groups of people, cities, governments, leaders and rulers, nations, etc.

There are multiple kinds of intercession, but here are seven categories of intercession that we have found to have the ability to tap into deeper wells in our lives:

1. Declaring faith and trust in the promises of God that He has made that have not yet been met/fulfilled.
2. Crying out for God's justice on behalf of others.
3. Crying out for God's mercy and grace on behalf of others.
4. Doing battle in the midst of spiritual warfare.
5. Calling upon God to reveal His nature, goodness, and power.
6. Passionately praying for someone else as if you were praying for yourself or for someone extremely close to you. This is called "identifying in intercession."
7. Prayer that goes beyond words, whether in the heavenly language of tongues or through the groaning of the Spirit within you.

Intercession has truly become a lost art. So much of regular prayer revolves around our needs and frustrations, with little to no listening as God speaks, as well as very little actual communion with Him. Intercession, to the vast majority of the Church, is misunderstood if it is even a thought at all. The Church—and the world—needs a resurgence of intercessors! We need men and women who will stand in the gap for our families, our neighbors and neighborhoods, our government and its leaders, our culture, and our cities and nation!

One of the most amazing truths about intercession is that when you begin to stand in the gap for others, God begins to work in you and transform you in great ways! Why do you think the Moravians became the leaders in world missions? Their commitment to community and intercession produced a movement that the world has rarely seen since—if at all!

Action Steps

1. Make 4 different lists—one for your family, one for someone that you know needs God, one for your community, and one for your nation.

2. On these lists, write down specific issues that need someone to "stand in the gap" for.

3. Begin interceding and standing in that gap, crying out for justice, mercy, grace, and hope. Pray for God's perfect will. Declare His goodness. As you pray, pay attention to the presence of the Holy Spirit and allow Him to guide you.

Contending/Warfare Prayer
The Prophetic Life of Prayer

$\mathcal{G}$rowing up in the Church, I had heard a lot about "spiritual warfare" and "warfare prayer." I was in every special service that our church hosted. I attended every revival week and listened to every guest speaker. During some of these services, there would be an emphasis on fighting the enemy with prayer and worship. Inevitably, people would begin praying loudly, crying out to God, and somebody would start playing Enemy's Camp and begin to "take back what he (the enemy) stole from me!" Some would march around the room in a symbolic "Jericho march." Whatever it looked like, that was my image of contending/warfare prayer. If you needed to do spiritual battle, it had to be loud, high energy, sweaty, and forceful. While I believe these may at times be part of warfare prayer, I think they are—like so many other things we do in Church—an expression of that form of prayer. I think contending prayer, or doing battle through prayer, is more than the expressions of prayer that many of us have experienced.

In Daniel 10, we find the prophet Daniel in the midst of praying and fasting for 21 days. He had just received a word from God about a great war. Deeply troubled by the vision he saw, he set himself to prayer and fasting to gain understanding. So impacted by this vision, the Bible states that Daniel was mourning.

For 20 days, without an answer, Daniel continued to pray. He longed for an answer to his prayers. He was troubled and disturbed by what he saw and why God would show it to him. Yet, he continued to pray.

Now, I don't know about you, but I have rarely prayed daily for a specific answer for more than a week, and when I have, it was typically a scheduled time of prayer and fasting. Daniel, however, begins his contending prayer session with no time frame attached. I believe that if it had taken 40 days to get an answer, he would have kept on keeping on! Nothing was going to stop him from receiving an answer from God.

On day 21, an angel arrives and speaks to Daniel. In every other account in the Bible, an angel will address the person and then deliver the message they have from God. But not here! The angel also adds some explanation to the delay in bringing the answer to Daniel's prayer. The angel says,

> "O Daniel, man greatly loved, understand the words that I speak to you; and stand upright, for now I have been sent to you...Fear not, Daniel, for from the first day that you set your heart to understand and humbled yourself before your God, your words have been heard, and I have come because of your words. The prince of the kingdom of Persia withstood me twenty-one days, but Michael, one of the chief princes, came to help me, for I was left there with the kings of Persia, and

came to make you understand what is to happen to your people in the latter days. For the vision is for days yet to come."[15]

I want to draw your attention to three things in the text. First of all, from the very first day that Daniel began praying, his prayers were heard, yet not answered. When you enter into prayer concerning troubling situations, events, etc…you must first take confidence in knowing that your prayers are immediately heard. There is never a time when God is not listening or ignoring your prayers. Never! If you understand that, keep reading!

Secondly, Daniel did not just begin praying based purely on his emotions. He set his heart to understand. To Jews, the heart was understood (and conveyed in the Hebrew language) as the seat of the mind, will, and emotions.. Daniel, motivated by his emotions and lacking understanding in his mind, engages his will as he enters into this period of warfare prayer. He sets his heart in place for the battle. I picture this determination like a warrior on a field, planting his feet in place and lifting his swords as he prepares to do battle with the enemy rushing towards him. Daniel was committed from the very onset to pray through this troubling situation until an answer came.

Third, Daniel also humbled himself as he set his heart to understand. Simply being stubborn about getting an answer will only lead to discouragement and arrogance, as if we can demand answers from our Creator! No—Daniel humbled himself, preparing himself to receive whatever answer God would provide, whether he liked it or not.

That was Daniel's spiritual posture for 21 days. For three weeks, Daniel contended—did spiritual battle—until the answer came. This is huge! Sometimes we need to fight with prayer the forces and

---

15 Daniel 10:11-14

situations that come against us. After all, "The weapons we fight with are not the weapons of the world. On the contrary, they have divine power to demolish strongholds" (2 Corinthians 10:4).

Action Steps

1. Reflect on a serious situation going on in your life or in the life of someone else. Determine if this is something you need to go to battle over.

2. Set a start day and time to begin doing spiritual warfare/ contending in prayer—commit and set your heart to see it through, humble yourself, and remember that your prayers are effective and always heard!

A Life of Faith
The Prophetic Life of Prayer (Darcie)

*Y*ou can never know you live by faith until it's tested. You can say, "I live by faith." But do you? There is a reason the Bible says to come in child-like faith.

Jesus said,

> *"Truly I tell you, unless you change and become like little children, you will never enter the kingdom of heaven."*[16]

Have you ever interacted with a child? They take you at your word. They believe in dreaming and imagination. They simply live life and take things as fact.

One night, my son was dealing with extremely itchy skin. We tried a lot of different lotions, took an oatmeal bath, but to no avail. I heard him crying my name and saying, "Mommy, bring me some mud. I need mud!" "Mud?" I asked. Yes, mud. He wanted me to rub mud

---

16 Matthew 18:3

all over his skin so that Jesus would heal him, just like he did for the blind man in the Bible. Oh, my heart! That is child-like faith!

I grew up with being confident of who God said he was. As a young girl, I took my mom's Bible and a special notebook. I found where she had written out the names of God. I couldn't even pronounce them, but I vividly remember copying each one on a loose-leaf paper, with a very potent, permanent black marker! I wanted to know God in the ways the Bible describes Him. I wanted to trust him completely. Little did I know how that one moment would impact the rest of my life.

To live a life of faith, you need to understand who God is. Life and all its circumstances will come and go, but God—our unchangeable God—is steadfast. His character does not lie. He is who He says He is! You won't be nervous about trusting a God who is peace. He is a comforter, a strong and safe tower. A God who provides, heals, and is the Great I AM—everything we could ever need!

When I was in third grade, I needed a costume for a school play. We didn't have the money just to go buy what was needed. My older sisters didn't have what I needed, either. I remember feeling just plain awful about the whole situation. Then, my mom said, "Darcie, go pray for it." And I did! The next day, we received a bag of clothes, and in it was *exactly* what I prayed for, even the exact color I wanted!

That was the starting point for my life of faith. I have prayed for little, unimportant things, and I have prayed for big needs that only God could do. I have seen God provide, heal, encourage, and protect me. I have learned that it isn't just a name it and claim it mentality. It is aligning yourself with the will of God. I have prayed, and the answers were not always what I had anticipated. Your prayer life is not a demanding attitude towards God. It is a "thy will be done" attitude.

Do you trust him enough to say, "God, I am willing to accept whatever you have for me?"

When I was in my senior year of high school, I had already known I was going to pursue full-time ministry as a career choice. I thought I was going to go to a 10-month discipleship program that was very hands-on. On a plane ride home from Phoenix, Arizona, I knew God was telling me that my plans were not going to happen. I was devastated. I didn't want to go to college. But God said, "Trust me!" On top of changing the direction of my training, I also felt God told me not to take out any school loans to pay for college. What?! I didn't even know if the college would allow me to "live by faith," even though it was a school that had started out in faith! But I obeyed. Talk about living by faith! With no backup plan, I asked the school to allow me to attend with insufficient funds and told them that I would willingly leave if I could not make the payments. They accepted these terms, and off I went.

God blessed the obedience of my heart and provided that first year of college. After two years off, I went back and continued the journey of living by faith. I remember that I had found dimes that whole summer before. I found them on the street, in my car, in my bedroom, in stores. I am telling you...*everywhere!* God spoke so directly to my heart. I felt him saying, "If you are faithful in your tithes *and* offerings, I will be faithful to you." Any time I felt tempted to withhold my tithe, I would find another dime! I kept obeying. I kept tithing and giving, and I kept paying off my school tuition little by little. Long story short, I graduated debt-free! Our God is not limited by our fears or our lack of resources. He takes what we have. We give Him a willing and obedient heart, and He creates a miracle.

I encourage you to live a life of faith and allow it to start in your prayer life. Pray big! Obey what he tells you to do. It may be something small and seemingly insignificant. Or maybe it is something that seems too big. You can only know if you are living a life of faith by testing it!

Action Steps

1. Think of the biggest need in your life. Pray for it like a child that asks for food, knowing nothing else but a good parent who would give it without hesitation.

2. Ask your Father if there are any areas in your life that He wants to challenge you in. Maybe it concerns a relationship, your finances, plans that you have, or something special that He wants you to do? Whatever it may be, open yourself to the voice of your loving Father. Hear Him and obey.

Spirit-Led Prayer
The Prophetic Life of Prayer

*T*his title seems somewhat redundant because prayer is typically Spirit-led, to begin with. But what I am talking about is a specific moment that can take place in prayer where although your mouth is moving and praying, you stop, and Holy Spirit takes over.

I was once in a prayer room with some other men. We all felt we needed to come and spend some time in prayer together. This prayer time started about as typical as these times do. We had some worship music playing through a phone, some of us were pacing while others were sitting, some of us were sitting quietly and getting our spirits to the place of rest while others were reading their Bibles, etc.

Eventually, we started praying. It flowed in and out of individuals praying and corporate praying. I remember the group coming to a quiet moment when nobody was praying, and the presence of God was thick and heavy. I felt impressed to begin praying. I didn't know what to pray for, but I knew I was supposed to start.

That was when something that had never happened to me

before took place. As I opened my mouth to pray, I felt one of the guys put their warm hands on my shoulders. And at that exact moment, words began flowing out of me that I was not fully conscious of speaking. I knew I was talking, but I was not thinking about what I was saying. It was as if a faucet had been turned on, and the water began flowing. My words were flowing out of my spirit. It was a prayer full of concepts and petitions that I had never thought of before, but turned out to be prophetic and extraordinarily accurate!

When I stopped praying, I immediately looked behind me to see which guy had his hands on me to thank him for praying for me. But nobody was there! Everyone in the room was in front of me. I physically felt two strong, warm hands rest and put pressure on my shoulders. I have no explanation for this except for I believe that an angel had touched me and supernaturally given me the message from the Lord that this angel wanted me to pray.

This type of experience is not uncommon throughout the Bible. Holy Spirit will come upon certain people, amid prayer, and begin communicating His heart and direction for prayer. Some examples are:

- Ananias—The Lord came in a vision and told him to go pray for healing over Saul, whom God had chosen to carry the Gospel to the Gentiles (Acts 9).
- Agabus—From scripture we can assume that Agabus, the New Testament prophet, was at a meeting of the church in Antioch. During this meeting, he stood up and began prophesying about the widespread famine that struck the entire Roman Empire, which led the believers there to take up a collection and send it to the believers in Judea (Acts 11).
- Commissioning of Saul & Barnabas—The church in Antioch

was worshipping, praying, and fasting, and in the midst of it, the Holy Spirit told them to commission Saul & Barnabas for the work the Lord had for them (Acts 13).

Holy Spirit is with you all the time, even when you pray. And He wants to speak through you—in life and in prayer. So the big question is: "How do you get to this place in prayer?" While Holy Spirit does as He wishes when He wishes, I believe there are a few helpful steps one can take to "clear the road" of any hindrances for Holy Spirit to speak:

Action Steps

The next time you are going to pray, try the following suggestions:

1. Silence/turn off your cell phone & any other electronic devices (If you can't just leave them behind).

2. Quiet your heart. Try not to designate prayer time right after watching television or a movie where your mind is unfocused.

3. Listen to worship music to help get your heart and spirit prepared.

4. Go somewhere secluded where you can be alone. A coffee shop, restaurant, or sitting area in a mall (and the like) are not the best options.

5. Make a mental list of all the stress, emotions, and frustrations you've been dealing with that day/week and then push it all away and far from your thoughts. Turn your thoughts towards God, what He has done, and look for that place of rest.

Plan & Purpose
Creative Beings

"God said, 'Let Us make man in Our image, according to Our likeness'...God created man in His own image, in the image of God He created him; male and female He created them." (Genesis 1:26-27)

*Y*ou were made in the very image and likeness of your Creator—God. Time out! Pause! Too many times, we blow right by this statement. You probably thought to yourself, "I know this...praise God...amen!" But we often do not consider the implications that come with such a statement and reality.

You see, you were made in the image and likeness of God, the Creator. If you were made in the likeness of the Creator, the implication is that you are also a creator. God designed Mankind to be creative beings—both male and female. All of human history, including the world we now live in, testify to this very truth. Our scientific and medical knowledge and practices have advanced incredibly! We have eliminated diseases that have wiped out whole populations. Our technology has advanced beyond anything ancient civilizations could have imagined. They controlled the ground, yet we have learned to control the skies! The list is endless concerning how the creative nature of Man has transformed the world!

But seemingly for most followers of Jesus, this creativity lies dormant. It is asleep, or worse yet, forgotten within. And yet, creative beings we have been fashioned to be. To deny this fact is to deny part of our very image/identity.

You're probably asking yourself right now, "What in the world does creativity have to do with prayer?" Nothing…and everything! Have I confused you enough yet? Yes?

Good!

It takes no creativity to live a life of prayer. The action of prayer itself takes very little (if any) creativity. Anyone can recite a prayer or a chant. But to pray with intentionality requires a degree of creativity. Think about it, as you pray, you are deciding what words/ statements to utter in your communication with God. That takes a measure of creativity. But that is where most Christians stop. They don't realize how much more there is to this creativity in prayer!

When you engage in intentional prayer, you—as a creative being made in the image of the Creator—are capable of thinking of creative solutions to pray about. You are able to allow a singular, simple thought God gives you to morph into an intricate, highly creative petition. Allow me to provide you with an example.

I once attended a church conference in New Haven, Connecticut. The emphasis was on the presence of God, and there were some fantastic, high-profile guest speakers lined up—mighty men and women of God.

I was attending this meeting with several friends. One of which

I was not too familiar with. We'll call her Megan. I did not know much about her, except for the fact that she always seemed depressed. She slept all the time, was typically pessimistic, wore dark clothing, brought all positive conversation to a screeching halt, seemed to think that nothing would ever go well, and could never muster anything but a weak and half-hearted smile.

Well, the service was amazing! God was really moving in the lives of people. Our group of friends decided to begin praying for each other. We all took turns being the one prayed for. I still clearly remember when we started praying for Megan. She was her typical sad self. We started praying, and the group was praying for all kinds of things, which were very encouraging.

All of a sudden, I had this image of Megan dancing wildly with the biggest smile on her face. As I saw this in my head, I had the name, "David" sound off in my mind as well. So I began praying. I prayed that a "spirit of David" would come upon her and set her free. I had never heard this term before (although I now know it is widely used in certain Church circles). I began praying more specifically and creatively as I was obedient to what I was shown.

As I prayed for her, I kept my eyes open (always do this!). I saw an incredibly beautiful transformation take place. It was as if the girl dancing in my mind came out and took over the sad, depressed version of Megan to whom we were all accustomed! She began dancing in worship before the Creator, who had set her free to be who He created her to be. From that day forward, because of a group of friends and the creativity they engaged with during prayer, she was the most positive, joyful person you could meet!

Don't neglect the creativity with which you have been created with. Engage it in prayer and allow God to use you in amazing—creative—ways!

Action Steps

1. Begin engaging your creativity in practical ways. The natural will often reveal the supernatural—engaging your innate creativity (no matter how that comes out) will help stir spiritual creativity in your life of prayer.

2. As you continue to pray for yourself, commune with God, or pray for others, begin trying to engage your creativity. Don't settle for the same generic prayers that we can often slip into praying. Use your creativity. It is a gift from God!

Plan & Purpose
Divine Appointments

$\mathcal{G}$od's intention for our walk with Him has never been to be solely "God-focused." Now, if that sounds strange, please keep reading so I can explain. God is our everything—He's the most important and central part of our lives. That is without question. But God is not content with us being only God-focused and not others-focused.

Jesus was once asked by an expert on the Law of Moses about which of God's commandments given to them was the greatest. Jesus answered that loving God and loving people summarized all of the Law and everything written to them by their Prophets.

God always wants us to be "others-minded"—showing compassion, representing Him well, revealing God's love for them through our lives, inviting others into an encounter with Him, spreading the Gospel, etc. We should always be intentional and active in this.

But there are times when God wants to set others up with perfect-precision to meet us so we can lead them into an encounter with their heavenly Father. We call this a divine appointment.

When I was in Bible college, I was part of a weekly street team—groups of students who would go out into the streets of downtown Providence, Rhode Island, and release the love and power of God as we witnessed and shared the Gospel. On one particular night, when the semester was over, several of us who were left decided to go out and see what God would have for us in the streets that night. We prayed for divine appointments.

I do not exaggerate when I say that for the next 4 hours, God set us up with many of these encounters. It was so perfect, it almost seemed too perfect, which is a trademark of a divine appointment. So many people came and approached us that night. So many we ran into were powerfully impacted by the presence of God! I have never experienced a night like that since, but desperately long for more!

The fact of the matter is that you will never meet every single person living in your community in a personal setting where you can build a relationship. It is impossible. Praying for and engaging in divine appointments cuts out this issue and allows us to have an impact wherever and whenever they come, with whomever we encounter!

The trick of it is identifying a divine appointment when it comes. As obvious as these moments can be at times, we can be so easily distracted and completely miss what God is trying to do in the midst of our jam-packed schedules! Here are some ways I have learned to be sensitive to when these opportunities come:

- Start each day with the Lord—get your heart aligned with His.
- Ask yourself this question each morning: "Who does God want me to meet today?" This will get you in the right mindset.

- Every time you walk into a new building, realize it is a new opportunity with a new group of people to whom you can reveal the love of God.

- Take regular and frequent pauses throughout the day to close your eyes and turn the gaze of your heart upon the Lord to realign yourself with His will and voice.

- Make these steps habitual. They will increase your ability to be aware throughout the day—even subconsciously—of God's presence, His will, and the divine appointments He has set for you.

Action Steps

1. Today (or tomorrow, depending on when you are reading this), make it a point to slow down your "hustle" and work at being much more aware of your surroundings, especially the people around you throughout the day.

2. Be on the lookout for opportunities the Lord may have orchestrated. Some common ones we have found are: cashiers, delivery men, neighbors, stock workers, bank tellers, people waiting in line with you, people with a visible physical impairment, homeless people on the side of the road with signs, broken down cars, doctors & nurses, waiters/waitresses, delivery people, teachers, coaches, etc.

3. If you find an opportunity—take it! Reveal the love of God!

Week 4 - Day 3
Plan & Purpose
Baptism in the Holy Spirit

*B*elonging to the charismatic, pentecostal lifestyle of Christianity, the baptism in the Holy Spirit is highly important to us. It is an essential part of this life that we are meant to live! Unfortunately, it is also a highly debated topic. Not so much on the existence of the baptism, but rather the effects it has on a believer.

But one thing that most of us can agree on is the purpose. JJesus, when He was leaving our world to take His place beside the Father, told His disciples about the coming of the Holy Spirit. He said,

> *"You will receive power when the Holy Spirit comes on you; and you will be my witnesses in Jerusalem, and in all Judea and Samaria, and to the ends of the earth."*[17]

Power. Witnesses. Work that reaches locally and to the ends of the earth. That is what the purpose of being baptized in the Holy

---

17 Acts 1:8

Spirit is all about. It is to give us a supernatural power to be effective witnesses to the world about what we have experienced about Jesus, grace, forgiveness, the Father, and His Kingdom.

This word for power, in the original language, refers to a power or ability to accomplish something. It is not a power given so it could lie dormant—untouched and untapped. This power to be effective witnesses has come to make us active in spreading the Good News of King Jesus and His Kingdom!

That was not the first time Jesus spoke of the Holy Spirit, however. In John 16:7, Jesus says,

> *"Nevertheless, I tell you the truth: it is to your advantage that I go away, for if I do not go away, the Helper (Comforter, Advocate) will not come to you. But if I go, I will send him to you…" (ESV).*

This word for "Helper, Comforter, or Advocate" is *paraklētos* in the original Greek. In New Testament times, this was a legal term referring to an attorney or lawyer. It is a person who can give the right evidence that can hold up in court because of their nearness to the situation.

Jesus also does not leave the matter by simply naming this *parakletos*. He speaks to what He will accomplish when He comes:

> *"When he comes, he will prove the world to be in the wrong about sin and righteousness and judgment: about sin, because people do not believe in me; about righteousness, because I am going to the Father, where you can see me no longer; and about judgment, because the prince of this world now stands*

condemned."[18]

Using appropriate courtroom language, Jesus states that Holy Spirit will prove (expose as guilty; convince with substantial, compelling evidence) that the world is guilty of sin, unrighteous, and judgment has been passed. But what was this judgment? It is two-fold. First of all, the world is guilty of sin and deserving condemnation, but the King has forgiven their great, impossible-to-pay debt and has shown them true grace, love, and acceptance into His Kingdom. Secondly, the one responsible for the condition of the world—Satan (accuser)—has been found guilty and has been condemned/sentenced.

This message is what the Holy Spirit empowers us to deliver effectively! And what a powerful message it is! When it comes to the plan and purpose God has for your life, it is so important to be baptized in the Holy Spirit. But do not be mistaken—this is not a one-time experience! We need to continually be refreshed with the Holy Spirit filling us to completion in our lives. It was God's intention from the beginning that we do not build His Kingdom on our own. We were always meant to have the Holy Spirit with us. Intimately close and powerfully moving through us!

Action Steps

1. Take some time during your time with God and ask the Holy Spirit to fill you.

---

18 John 16:8-11

2. Make sure your mindset is, "God, you can have all of me if I can have all of you!"

3. Understand that once you became a follower of Jesus, Holy Spirit has already taken up residence inside of you. The baptism is Him rising within you immeasurably more, like a person being immersed in water until he is fully covered.

Plan & Purpose
Boldness (Darcie)

*T*he New Testament instructs us that we are called to be bold in our faith, in our beliefs, and our prayer life. In the Old Testament, as the Israelites were about to enter into the Promised Land and a major military campaign, Joshua was told not to be afraid, but rather to be bold and courageous, because God was with them.

Boldness is counter-intuitive for humans because many of us do not like what we consider to be conflict. Some people seem to like conflict, but the problem is that those who appear this way are not really feeling the stress of the conflict, so it does not actually become a conflict for them. Instead, they seem to enjoy it. However, there are certain situations that they would consider to be conflict, and I guarantee that they would not like it at all! Because we naturally like comfort and peace as human beings, conflict upsets us and is extremely uncomfortable. The most natural way to deal with this is to avoid conflict or dismiss it as soon as possible, no matter what the cost. Boldness, therefore, is counter-intuitive. But boldness is so necessary to the life of a follower of Jesus, as well as to living a life of prayer.

Instead of justifying our lack of boldness by viewing it as something that only "special" people are born with, we must realize that every follower of Jesus has been instructed in the Bible to be bold. Here are some verses about that very instruction:

- "For God gave us a spirit not of fear but of power and love and self-control." (2 Timothy 1:7).
- "The wicked flee when no one pursues, but the righteous are bold as a lion" (Proverbs 28:1).
- "Because of Christ and our faith in him, we can now come boldly and confidently into God's presence" (Ephesians 3:12).
- "So let us keep on coming boldly to the throne of grace..." (Hebrews 4:16).

For a believer, boldness is the strength to do what is right and to speak what God has directed you to say. One of my favorite quotes about boldness is by a man named Edwin Cole, "Prayer in private results in boldness in public." Andrew Murray also said about boldness, "Boldness in prayer comes when I am assured that the spirit of asking and the thing I ask for are both according to the will of God."

Boldness and fear cannot exist at the same time. There is always a transition that takes place between being afraid and being bold. But they cannot co-exist. You can be fearful or intimidated in a situation, but to be bold requires that you push past the fear and remove its hold on you.

I grew up in an extremely rough neighborhood in Pittsburgh, Pennsylvania. Guns, gangs, drugs, and violence were normal in my neighborhood. One day when I came home, there was a group of about eight men gathered at the foot of the steps that led up to our house. There was no way to avoid them. Fear took over! But I soon felt the Lord's presence and immediately knew that I was safe and nothing would happen to me. With this newfound confidence and boldness, I strode up the steps and past this group to enter my home.

When it comes to God's plan and purposes for our lives, boldness is a necessary ingredient. We have been called by God to take this Gospel to all nations—to all people. Boldness is not merely a suggestion but a requirement if we are to fulfill this calling! Engaging a world with a message that is counter-to-culture produces conflict as a natural byproduct. It is only with boldness that we can see the building of God's Kingdom "on Earth as it is in Heaven" through to the end. We can, both in our prayers and our lives, learn and grow to be righteously bold and confident in what God desires to do through us. We can pray with a knowing that God will do as He says. We can walk into the worst situations with confidence that God will not only protect us but give us victory. We can face the greatest odds with boldness, understanding that God always has us covered! Fear is not of God. Don't allow the enemy to strangle you with the grip of intimidation and deny you everything that God has for you in this life!

Be bold, my friends!

Action Steps

1. There are most likely things that you felt God spoke to you that you gave up on due to fear or intimidation. In your prayer

time, boldly pray about these things again.

2. Part of being bold is to "materialize" instead of "internalize." You have to force yourself to do something bold instead of being passive. Stretch yourself. The next time God speaks to you about saying/doing something—think of a way to make it materialize and become tangible. Otherwise, it will stay inside and die.

Plan & Purpose
Perseverance

"Consider it pure joy, my brothers and sisters, whenever you face trials of many kinds, because you know that the testing of your faith produces perseverance. Let perseverance finish its work so that you may be mature and complete, not lacking anything. If any of you lacks wisdom, you should ask God, who gives generously to all without finding fault, and it will be given to you. But when you ask, you must believe and not doubt, because the one who doubts is like a wave of the sea, blown and tossed by the wind. That person should not expect to receive anything from the Lord. Such a person is double-minded and unstable in all they do." (James 1:2-7)

I want you to imagine that you are a 1st-century follower of Jesus, during the first few decades after Jesus has died, resurrected, and ascended into Heaven—charged with spreading the Gospel to the entire known world of the Roman Empire. Now I want you to imagine not only accomplishing this task but simply living as a Christian under the extreme persecution of both the Jews and the Romans. To both groups, you are an illegal religion. Such persecution has forced the known Church into being an underground Church to some extent. Punishments under this persecution include being stoned, beaten, whipped, flogged, arrested, imprisoned, attacked by mobs of people, and even executed.

These are the conditions under which James writes to the Church. In his epistle (letter), James chooses one subject to set the stage for his entire message: perseverance.

Trials and difficult situations—especially those that seem to stand in opposition to your walk as a follower of Jesus—are a fact of life. It appears that, especially in our culture today, that Christianity is under a massive attack. While it may be true that in we are not under the threat of death or imprisonment in the United States, the attack is still fierce—it is an attack against biblical truth and the very image of God, using words, emotions, and theories to tear apart the Church.

James is telling us that when we face trials, in whatever form they come, we are to consider it a joy because they are producing perseverance in us, which could not be produced otherwise. Perseverance is not a patience that passively endures, but rather is the image of a man standing his ground in defiance of a storm, refusing to be moved. It is a stick-to-it, dogged determination to push through whatever trial you face to see the power and glory of God shine through on the other side of the situation. Once you get to the other side, having persevered, you then have acquired a newfound strength and spiritual maturity.

But then James says something interesting. While you are persevering, you need wisdom. James infers that it is not a select few who need wisdom during trials, but *all* followers of Christ that need wisdom. Wisdom for what? Wisdom to persevere! This wisdom, which God is more than willing to give generously, is, in all actuality, a giving of perspective. It is the wisdom to see the big picture—to understand what is happening in your life and the lives of others. This is God-given wisdom to see the situation from God's point of view. And once you have this wisdom and understand what God will accomplish using what the enemy intended for evil, that warrior-like refusal to crumble to such trials and situations will surge within you and provide a newfound strength.

Newfound perseverance!

There are times in our lives when we feel as if our prayers are not being heard. We believe, have faith, keep our heads down and push through, but feel empty and alone. This creeping feeling of defeat and hopelessness is the exact moment that you need to set aside time to seek God and pursue that wisdom for perseverance!

I was once in the middle of a transition between ministries. My family was stressed, struggling, and hurting. We were pushing through, but it was taking a toll on us. So I decided I needed to seek God on our family's behalf. I took three days off of work and spent each day, from sun-up to sun-down, in a spare room in our house. I had one purpose: To fast, pray, and seek the presence and wisdom of God. Sure enough, He was faithful to answer! He gave us perspective. He gave us wisdom. He gave us the ability to persevere until we saw our lengthy transition end, and His next steps for us come to fruition!

No matter what situation(s) you are facing no matter how your faith is tested—I encourage you today to persevere! Don't give up! Don't give in! Deny the enemy the control over you that he seeks. Persevere!

Action Steps

1. Read the following verses: 1 Timothy 4:16; Hebrews 10:36; Romans 5:3-4; Hebrews 12:1-3.

2. On a piece of paper, write/type a statement that states your rejection of the notion of bowing to the trial/situation you are facing or will face. Post it somewhere you will see it. You may even want to print or write out the verses mentioned above to post as well!

Week 4 - Day 6
Plan & Purpose
Becoming Who You Were Created to Be

"*W*ho do you think you are, mister?" my dad said, obviously frustrated with my disobedience and disrespect. I mean…he called me *mister*! Things just got serious! My dad always tells this story with a huge smile, though, because of my reaction as a young child. "Who do you think you are, mister?" he said. And with tear-filled eyes ready to unleash their floodwaters, I responded, "I'm EJ, your *son*! Don't you know me?!"

As a parent, I have found myself asking this same question to my children (although I leave off the mister part). Who do you think you are? The question implies that the person/child is not acting as they should be. The question also implies that there is a version of us that we are supposed to be—a proper and inherent version of ourselves that we are to live out.

In Jeremiah 1:5, God says to the prophet Jeremiah,

"Before I formed you in the womb I knew you, before you

were born I set you apart; I appointed you as a prophet to the nations."

Some versions of this verse translate the word "knew" as "chose." But this changes the meaning of God's word entirely! The actual word translates to mean "knew." This word is a special Hebrew word that means to know someone or something through experience with it—experiential knowledge. God did not merely choose Jeremiah before He formed him in his mother's womb; God *knew* Jeremiah. That means that God had lovingly created Jeremiah with an intentional, planned image in mind. So detailed and so deep was this experience that God had fully known Jeremiah before he was even born! And it was not a purposeless existence to which he was created, but a life full of purpose and destiny! He set Jeremiah apart before he was born to be a prophet!

The simple truth is that God has lovingly, tenderly, powerfully, and intricately created every one of us with an incredible life, purpose, and destiny to live. He made us in His image! He gave us our emotions and personality. He walks with us through the situations we face in life so that we come out on the other side stronger and more like the ultimate version of us that He has created us to become.

But it is all too obvious in our day and age that many people, including Christians, do not walk according to who they were created to be. Many people settle for "good enough." Many people accept defeat and live their lives in a way that is minimally acceptable to themselves. Some have allowed situations and people to twist who they are, which they accept as their "lot in life." Still, others refuse to surrender their will to God and allow Him to lead them into a better life. As we have discussed before, identity is so important!

101

So the question for all of us is this: How do you become who you were created to be? Again, let's turn to what the Bible says:

"Do not conform to the pattern of this world, but be transformed by the renewing of your mind. Then you will be able to test and approve what God's will is—his good, pleasing and perfect will."[19]

The answer to becoming who we were created to be is to allow Holy Spirit to come and renew our minds—to bring a transformation to our thinking, thought-patterns, and way of viewing God and life. It is a quite literal change and metamorphosis that your mind goes through. The result of such a work is the ability to "test and approve what God's will is." This term test comes from a word that means to prove something as genuine.

Think of a historian reviewing a newly-discovered piece of an ancient document that has historical significance. He will run tests, research what he knows of the original document, and use his experience with the original to compare this new discovery. Because of his experience—his knowledge of the original—he is either able to approve or deny the genuineness of the newly found document. That is the picture the apostle Paul is trying to convey about what the renewing of our minds will enable within us. Because of this renewing of our minds, we can understand who God is, what He is truly like, and who He created us to be. Then and only then can we take steps towards becoming who God destined us to be. Without this renewal, we will find ourselves only falling prey to conforming to the ways of this world over and over again.

---

19 Romans 12:2

Action Steps

1. The next time you sit down to pray, set aside everything you think you know about yourself. Ask God to renew your mind. He may do this instantly, or you may need to pursue this for several days, if not longer, so don't be discouraged!

2. Whatever God reveals to you in your prayer time, or through reading the Bible, write it all down! Hang onto that list so you can go back to it over and over again. Add to it over time as God continues to renew your mind.

Plan & Purpose

Riding the Current

*T*he Voyage of St. Brendan of Ireland is one of my favorite stories in Church History. He is considered the Catholic patron saint of sailors. St. Brendan, along with several fellow monks, undertook a great voyage in an Irish boat called a coracle (currach). After about 15 days, the wind died out. The monks set themselves to the oars and paddled, but were soon out of strength. St. Brendan began to speak to his men. Carl Selmer records Brendan's words in his book, *Brendan the Navigator*: "'Brothers, do not fear, for God is our helper, our helmsman and our pilot, and He shall guide us. Pull in all the oars and the rudder. Just leave the sails spread, and let God do as He wishes with His servants and their boat.' Then they continued to refresh their strength until the evening, as long as the wind did not cease to blow. Still, they could not tell from which direction the wind came or in which direction the boat was carried."

There are also other stories from the Celtic Church about monks who felt led by the Spirit to get in their boats, and without sails or paddles, allow the currents to take them to wherever God wanted them to go to minister the Gospel.

These are incredible stories of faith! I don't know about you, but I am a pretty stick-to-the-plan kind of guy. Sure, I love adventure and walking into the unknown at times, but these stories take faith to an entirely new level! I mean, these were easily life-or-death situations in the middle of the ocean! And yet, God honored the faith of these men.

I think that most of you are probably like me. We like our plans. We like knowing the details. You may even like the unknown and surprises in life. But big faith risks? Those are few and far between in our lives.

But there are times when God is not going to ask you to go down a path that He reveals to you, but instead will simply ask you to go and *show you nothing*. We can look at these stories in the Celtic Church and call it "riding the current." I call it "walking in the darkness of God."

Let me explain.

The Bible, in several places, depicts God as a Being surrounded or shrouded in thick clouds—darkness. Here are a few of these verses:

- "The people remained at a distance, while Moses approached the thick darkness where God was." (Exodus 20:21)
- "These are the commandments the Lord proclaimed in a loud voice to your whole assembly there on the mountain from out of the fire, the cloud and the deep darkness…" (Deuteronomy 5:22)
- "Clouds and thick darkness surround Him…" (Psalm 97:2)

There are two basic categories that the word darkness falls into in the Bible: evil and the unknown. Obviously, when I refer to the "darkness of God" I am not saying that God is evil. I am talking about the unknown, mysterious side of following God.

When Moses and the Israelites had come to Mt. Sinai and were camped out, God spoke to Moses to prepare the people to meet with Him on the mountain on which He has descended. When they had consecrated themselves and the time had come, all the people approached the mountain. The way the Bible describes this mountain in Exodus 20 looks a lot like Mount Doom from the Lord of the Rings! Darkness in the sky, fire on the mountaintop, and thick and deep dark cloud descending the mountain where the presence of God would be waiting for them.

At the last moment, the people gave in to their fears and insecurities and told Moses to be their negotiator. Moses strides into the darkness and meets with God. But interestingly, when we read about Moses coming down to find the Israelites had made their famous golden calf idol, the text records that Joshua—Moses' aid—was with him! And who did God choose as Moses' successor?

Joshua!

God loves to reveal things about Himself and our lives to us! God loves to work through us to minister to the people all around us. We work hard to build His Kingdom and do our best to do so with excellence. We seek God and follow our Spirit-led plans. But sometimes, God does not want to reveal anything. He wants you to run into the cloud. He wants you to "go…to the land that I will show you" (Genesis 12:1, ESV) without showing you anything first!

This kind of faith is intimidating, and honestly quite scary. But it is also absolutely necessary for you to learn how to trust Him if you are going to accomplish your God-given plan and purpose in life! Jesus Himself praised those who would believe without having to see evidence for what they were to believe. Some of the greatest stories of faith have nothing to do with plans, and everything to do with the willingness to ride the current.

Action Steps

1. Think about your walk with the Lord—do you remember any time when you felt God was asking you to do something, but it was too scary for you? Or maybe He didn't give you enough details to provide you with the confidence in deciding to obey?

2. Once you think of one such instance, ask yourself: What kept me from going through with what it was that I felt God was leading me to do?

3. As you enter into your prayer time with God, do not pray for courage, faith, boldness, or obedience. Pray that God would open your eyes and heart to trust Him more. Lack of trust is the root of why we do not follow through with what God may ask us to do.

4. Ask God to make you more sensitive to His leading through-out the day.

5. As you go about your day, pay special attention to the still, small voice of God speaking to you—He may just ask you to take that step of faith, ride the current, and walk into the darkness of God.

Building the Kingdom
The Gift of Faith (Darcie)

*A*s a pastor, I find that the spiritual gift of faith is understood by few and sought after by even less. I also think that we misunderstand what this gift of faith is all about. There is a difference between the gift of *saving* faith, which is given to all believers, and the *gift of the Spirit* called faith.

The gift of faith is a spiritual gift that enables a person to be so consumed with the conviction that God will do as He said He would do in a given situation. That covers a wide variety of topics, from finances, healing, miracles, signs & wonders, following God's plan to fruition, deliverance, resurrections, etc.

But faith is not about sitting by and waiting for something to happen. As we have already discussed, there are moments of perseverance in prayer that utilizes our faith, but faith is not limited to these situations alone. James, the brother of Jesus, writes,

"But someone will say, 'You have faith and I have works.'

Show me your faith apart from your works, and I will show you my faith by my works. You believe that God is one; you do well. Even the demons believe—and shudder! Do you want to be shown, you foolish person, that faith apart from works is useless?"

James is saying here that our faith in God should produce good works in our lives. This truth is key to understanding the more distinct gift of faith. The gift of faith enables us not only to have supernatural confidence to believe that God will do what He promised/revealed/ what we pray for, but that we will do our part in working to see the fulfillment of our faith come to fruition.

Here is a perfect example: My sister, RainyDawn, was once the assistant director of the Baltimore Master's Commission. One year, when I was about 15, this Master's Commission was organizing a mission trip to Honduras. I felt very strongly that I needed to go on this trip. So I signed up and began the fundraising journey. I worked hard to raise all of my funds to the best of my ability. One day before the trip, however, I was just under $200 short of what I needed to go on the trip. I was conflicted because I knew I didn't have the money, and my parents didn't have the money, but I felt so strongly that God wanted me to go on this trip. So, in faith, I drove down from Pittsburgh to Baltimore as if I was going on the trip. I was confident that God was going to provide. When I arrived, my sister took me to her friend's house for dinner. This friend's dad did not know my story or my need. We had never met before. After dinner, the dad came to me and asked me if I had all the money for the trip. When I told him that I did not have the money I needed for the trip, he told me that he felt God was telling him to pay for the rest of my trip! As if that was not amazing enough, he also gave me extra spending money! God did not just provide what I needed, but provided an abundance!

I tell you that story to tell you this: when you know that God asks you to do something, do it. When there is an impossible need, believe God for it and start doing something about it, in faith, to see it come to pass. One of my favorite quotes on the subject of faith is by the missionary Hudson Taylor: "God's work done in God's way will never lack God's supply." If you are pursuing the things that are important to God, then you can expect from Him that He will equip you with everything you need to meet that need.

Action Steps

1. It's time to think big! What is a significant need in your life or in the life of another? It needs to be something that you thought seemed impossible!

2. As you spend time with God, do not pray about the need. Instead, seek the gift of faith. Paul tells us to seek after the gifts eagerly. Why? Because we are supposed to have and use them!

3. Read Scriptures that talk about the faithfulness of God during your prayer time. This will help build your faith to trust Him for that big need!

4. You will begin to feel your faith grow. One of several indi-

cators will be that your "big" issue will not seem as big as it did before. This is not your need diminishing, but your faith increasing! Once this happens—pray with wild passion and trust!

5. After you have prayed, consider if there is anything you can do to act upon your faith. Maybe you need to initiate a conversation to reconcile a relationship? Maybe you need to attack your debt to get that house you've always dreamed of? Maybe you need to sit down and brainstorm about that book you felt God wanted you to write? Engage your faith by putting it into action!

6. This week, buy a good quality journal—this is your new faith journal. From now on, record every time God fulfills a promise, your faith is confirmed by God, He does a miracle/ healing, etc. You can go back to this repeatedly in the future when you need to build your faith.

Week 5 - Day 2
Building the Kingdom
Words of Knowledge

*L*ike many of the gifts of the Spirit, there is very little practical, "how-to" information or teachings on words of knowledge in scripture. The apostle Paul tells us to pursue the gifts eagerly, but gives us very few details about them. What I know about the gifts comes from what I have been taught by those who function in them, what we can infer from Scripture, and from my own experience.

The *word of knowledge* is a "knowing" of information that has not been naturally, but supernaturally revealed to a believer. This information can be about situations, memories, physical/spiritual issues, God's will, other people, nations, groups of people, and much more.

Words of knowledge have been one of the greatest tools for seeing the supernatural invade our natural world in my life. I have witnessed healing, salvation, deliverance, faith, and wonder come out of this gift of the Spirit.

I was once in a service where an evangelist was speaking. This man was particularly known for having a powerful word of knowledge gift. Towards the end of the service, he called out to a man in the audience and asked him to stand. He told the man that 25 years ago, this man was standing on a loading dock at a warehouse, finishing loading up a light blue delivery truck. And as this truck drove off, this man stared at it and said to God, "There has to be more than this. This can't be what I'm supposed to do with my life!" Then, this evangelist asked the man if he remembered this moment. With tears in his eyes, he nodded that he did remember. Wow! So specific! And the evangelist encouraged the man with what God wanted to say about that memory.

One of my first encounters with the word of knowledge gift was when I was on that mission trip to Jamaica in 2007. We were invited to speak to the students at the University of the West Indies in their chapel building. Our trip leader (who also had a strong word of knowledge gift) gave each of us on the team a 5-minute window to speak. He also asked us to ask God for five specific words of knowledge. I had never received a word of knowledge before, and it sounded odd to me, but I decided to do it anyway. After a few minutes of prayer, I had what I thought God had spoken to me.

After we had all preached, our leader got up and began to call out all of these words of knowledge. I was shocked by the response! Every…single…one of our words were accurate! We began praying for people in that place and saw healing, deliverance, and joy! There was an intense sense of the presence of the Lord in that place that day as lives were changed, and God made Himself tangibly known!

And that is exactly what the gifts of the Spirit are all about—God making Himself known! These gifts are not to be used for self gain (although, sadly, there have been many who have done so). They are not to be conjured up and used to manipulate people. They are to reveal God's will and love for His people. Period.

What is vital for you to understand is that the word of knowledge is not for some super-holier-than-thou-mega-believer. It is accessible to *all* believers. If you love Jesus and desire to be used by Him, then you qualify to function in the gift of words of knowledge! It takes time and training, but it can be done!

But like any of these gifts, it requires a level of risk. You have to be willing to fail and "miss it." We learn many times from our failures more than from our successes. The willingness to be used by God, and to be humble enough to get it wrong, are the keys to being used in words of knowledge!

Action Steps

1. Make up your mind here and now if you want God to use you in the gift of the Spirit.

2. If you do, then pursue it. Ask God to awaken that gift within you.

3. When you feel like God may be speaking to you a word of knowledge, take a risk and act on it (Only one word of caution—use tact in acting upon any of the gifts. God cares more about you using them in love and respect than He does about you being right!)

Building the Kingdom
Word of Wisdom

*I*f the word of knowledge has been misunderstood, then the word of wisdom has been downright confusing! There are very few teachings on the spiritual gifts, and especially the *revelatory* gifts, of which the word of wisdom is one.

We find the word of wisdom listed among several other spiritual gifts in 1 Corinthians 12:8,

> *"To one there is given through the Spirit a message of wisdom, to another a message of knowledge by means of the same Spirit."*

By including the words "by means of the same Spirit," the apostle Paul links both *words of knowledge* and *words of wisdom* together. Many times these two gifts may function together in partnership to accomplish God's perfect will in a situation.

The word of wisdom has more to do with interpretation than it does information. It is explanatory in nature. A word of wisdom comes to do one of two things: (1) Interpret dreams, visions, etc. (2) Provide knowledge/insight into what is required for righteous actions or living and for building God's Kingdom on Earth.

You can have wisdom from God and be considered wise by those around you, and yet not function in the word of wisdom gift. Wisdom is analyzing a situation and understanding what the mind of God would decide and then acting upon it. The word of wisdom is interpreting things that are mysterious/unknown (dreams & visions), and instructing someone (even yourself, if you are the dreamer) about decisions, situations, relationships, finances, etc.

The reason both of these gifts get so confused is because they are both revelatory and can sometimes touch each other in the same situation. Allow me to provide a few examples of them individually, as well as when they work together.

I had mentioned before that I had an extremely vivid dream once that ended up being God telling me about going on a mission trip to Jamaica. When I had this dream, I was so confused! So I went seeking counsel from friends who had more experience than I did. They spoke to me and gave me what they felt the Lord was saying. Everything they said was amazing but wrong! I had this "knowing" on the inside of me that what they were telling me was wrong. It just was not sitting well with me. It felt like trying to force a puzzle piece into the wrong spot. Afterward, I was walking away when another friend (who was present but did not give his opinion) came up to me and told me what he felt God was saying through my dream. This time I knew he was right on target! Everything made sense. Not only that, but my dream actually came true according to how he interpreted it with scary accuracy! This is one example of a word of wisdom!

During one of our church services at Connect Church, I felt God was speaking to me during our worship time. I felt God pinpoint in my body a pain that someone was having in their spine. It was a precise location. I took out my phone and looked up the medical identifications of the vertebrae. I felt the issue was between the T3 and T4 vertebrae. When I called this out, a lady came forward and said she had been involved in a terrible car accident a few years before and was miraculously still alive. She had several medical issues from this accident, including a spinal disk issue. Can you guess between which vertebrae the injured disk was located? T3 and T4—exactly! This is an example of the word of knowledge.

As I said, sometimes, these two gifts function together. I once was in a seminar where a man singled me out of the room full of people and began speaking into my life. He told me that when I was around 11 or 12 years old, the enemy tried to kill me because of the calling that was on my life. He then told me that the Lord protected me and has stood guard over me ever since. After this he gave me further instructions as to the purpose God had for my life, and why He had saved me. There was a time when I was 11 or 12 years old when I was snowboarding at a friend's New Year's Day party. Everyone was going down the same steep path on a really steep hill in his back-yard while the parents were all inside the house. When it came to my turn, I stepped onto the cheapest, slip-on snowboard and started going down the hill. As I started going faster and faster, I suddenly found myself flying through the air upside-down. To this day, I have no idea what I hit on the path. It was the same path everyone else was riding, but I struck something, and the front of my snowboard got stuck and launched me into the air, out of my boots. I landed directly on my head and felt a sickening snap in my neck. The next few moments were a blur as I tried to move my body. I could breathe, but could not move anything below my neck. I knew that I had damaged my neck severely if not broken it all together! I began praying desperately, and in a few moments, I sat upright, completely fine. I knew this was the occasion this man was talking about.

The word of knowledge was the revealing of the event of my accident. The word of wisdom was the revealing of the work of the enemy, God's protection on my life, and what I was to do about it. This is one of the many dynamic examples of these two gifts working together in life and ministry.

Action Steps

1. Get with a group of believers who are also seeking the gifts of the Spirit.

2. Begin to worship and praise God in a time of prayer. Then sit one person in the middle of the group and begin asking God privately for a word of knowledge for that person. Then, whether you receive something or someone else does, ask for a word of wisdom.

3. The next time somebody tells you about a dream they had, ask God if it is from Him, and if so, ask for Him to give you the word of wisdom/interpretation of the dream.

4. Rule #1 of all the gifts of the Spirit—They are all to be used

to encourage and to show God's love! Do not deliver any message that is full of condemnation or pessimism.

Building the Kingdom
Prophecy

*I*f any subject has been more taboo in the Church in recent history, it has been the subject of prophecy. There have been so many prophecies given—especially concerning eschatological, "end-of-the-world" events. Most of us can remember the several false end-of-the-world prophecies that have been given or made famous in recent years: The Mayan calendar ending in 2012, September 23 of 2015 (which was then switched to October 23 of 2015 once September came and went and the world was still here), the several false prophecies published by the Jehovah Witnesses, etc. Some of the newest ones deal with "blood moons" and the prophetic comparisons of different world leaders to major players in the end-times narrative. Many well-intentioned ministers and their recent writings concerning prophecy and end-times events have, in my opinion, severely damaged, if not destroyed, the credibility of legitimate prophecy in the Church.

Despite the errors of others, who have torn apart the reputation of the gift of prophecy, the truth is that prophecy is not only a legitimate gift of the Spirit, but a necessary gift for today! The challenge is in understanding this gift so we can use it properly and effectively.

When the apostle Paul gives a list of some of the gifts of the Spirit in 1 Corinthians, he uses the Greek word *prophēteúō*, which means "forthtelling a revelation of the mind/message of God." It can also mean "foretelling the future as God reveals it."

There is a lot of confusion as to how this gift is supposed to function. The problem is rooted in the examples we see in Scripture, specifically between the prophets of the Old Testament and the prophets of the New Testament. In the Old Testament, much of the messages given by the prophets were judgment-centered. They dealt with the sins of people and nations that breached God's covenant with His people. As a result, these prophecies often foretold the covenantal judgment that was coming. The Old Testament records much less frequently the times when a prophet had a message to deliver that was encouraging. In the New Testament, however, the opposite seems to be true of the prophet. They were first and foremost encouragers and exhorters! The messages that they delivered were given in love and were always meant to encourage, build-up, and strengthen people! The gift of prophecy was *not* meant to tear down anyone, bring accusations, or pronounce judgment. Jesus paid the price for *all* sin and took away *all* condemnation! Remember what Paul wrote:

> *"God was reconciling the world to himself in Christ, not counting people's sins against them…"*[20]

When Jesus died on the cross and was raised back to life, God stopped counting our sins against us. Salvation is not based on

---

20 2 Corinthians 5:19

works—what we do or don't do. It is based on grace alone. And grace can only be produced through relationship. It is our relationship with God that is the determining factor! And relationships never grow through condemnation, accusation, piling on guilt, or judgmental words. Relationships grow through encouragement, self-sacrifice, exhorting, reconciliation, love, and grace!

The role of the spiritual gift of prophecy is, therefore, always one of encouragement. I would even go so far as to say that if someone utters a message meant to be prophetic that is full of judgment and condemnation, that it is not from God. I am not saying prophecy cannot point out sin, poor choices, rebellion, etc. Far from it! But it must always have a core message of encouragement, fueling the rest of the prophecy.

I once had a man prophesy over me that I would be asked to lead a group of young people on a mission trip. Shortly after this prophetic word, I received a random call from a friend asking me to lead a group of young adults on a mission trip with their group!

I was leading a church service once when, all of a sudden, I had a random image of the nation of China appear in my mind. As soon as I thought it, I felt the impression of the word "missions." So I said, "There is someone in this room who God has spoken to you about doing missions work in China, but you have fought and struggled with it. But God is telling you to go!" After service, a young adult woman found me and told me she had an opportunity to go on a missions trip to China, but because of the cost of the trip (and naturally being quite intimidated by such an undertaking), she had been putting it off. She determined to obey God and go, and God did amazing things through her faithfulness!

Prophecy gives us the incredible opportunity to speak life, encouragement, and grace into people's lives. It affords us the ability to change the course of people's lives as we lead them closer to God and closer to the plan and purpose He has for their lives! That is why Paul encourages us to, "Follow the way of love and eagerly desire gifts of the Spirit, especially prophecy" (1 Corinthians 14:1).

Action Steps

1. When you receive a word of prophecy, you will typically be able to identify it by the overwhelming urge to deliver it and the weight that it sits in your heart and spirit.

2. Again, there are several ways to receive a word of prophecy. Some of these include impressions, random thoughts, images, visions, and dreams.

3. It is important to remember that you are in control. You have control over when you share it and how you share it. The "spirit is subject to the prophet," not the other way around. Always wait for appropriate timing to share in a service that does not disrupt the flow of the service.

4. When sharing a word of prophecy with someone in a private setting, do so with all of the tact, respect, and love you can muster. Prophecy is freaky enough when it is accurate…no need to make it worse by bad timing, horrible delivery, and a bunch of "Christianese" that will mean nothing to the person

with whom you are speaking.

Building the Kingdom
Alignment

*M*any people do not realize the importance of alignment when it comes to life, ministry, and prayer. When we talk about alignment, we are not talking about the steering of your car. We are talking about aligning under our authorities. Certain leaders have horribly abused the subjects of authority and submission in churches who seem to think that their authority is to be used to demand loyalty, financial support, obedience without question, and a form of leader-worship. They use their position of leadership as a means to promote themselves and their agendas. Leaders who do this fancy themselves above others and expect to be treated like royalty. As a result, these poor examples of leadership have only birthed a generation of people who do not truly understand authority and have even, at times, given in to an attitude of rebellion.

Despite this abuse of authority and alignment, the fact remains that God has ordered our world, and the Church, by giving us all authorities to align ourselves beneath. Authority is one of the main ways through which God brings spiritual growth and equips us to live our lives according to His plan and purpose.

Think about this: the only person in Jesus' entire life and ministry that He was ever impressed with because of their faith was a Roman centurion (soldier). The Romans were the invading army in Israel in Jesus' day. They were the *enemies!* They were the ones that many people believed and hoped that the Messiah would come and defeat—not to be impressed with! Why was Jesus impressed with a pagan warrior? Because he understood authority! Listen to the words of this centurion as He reveals His understanding and faith simultaneously to Jesus:

> *"...The centurion sent friends to say to him (Jesus): 'Lord, don't trouble yourself, for I do not deserve to have you come under my roof. That is why I did not even consider myself worthy to come to you. But say the word, and my servant will be healed. For I myself am a man under authority, with soldiers under me. I tell this one, "Go," and he goes; and that one, "Come," and he comes. I say to my servant, "Do this," and he does it.'"*[21]

As a soldier, this centurion understood the structure and flow of authority within the military. You do not question orders. Military leaders with authority know that when they speak a command, they do not have to wonder if their command will be obeyed—they expect it with great certainty! On the off-chance that a soldier did choose to disregard an order given by someone with authority over them, it was viewed as rebellion towards caesar himself! Caesar was the source of

---

21 Luke 7:6-8

the centurion's authority. To disrespect him was to disrespect caesar.

The same is true when we talk about authority in the Kingdom of God and how that impacts our world. Romans 13:1 states,

> *"...There is no authority except that which God has established. The authorities that exist have been established by God."*

All authority is established and given to us by God. And how we show honor and respect—as well as how we bring ourselves into proper alignment under such authorities—determines the flow of blessings and favor from God in our lives. And to show disrespect and disregard for our authorities is as if we are showing disrespect and disregard for God Himself!

But Pastor EJ—what about leaders who abuse their power or use it to do great evil? Surely they are not deserving of our respect? Actually, yes, they are. The apostle Peter once wrote, "Respect everyone, and love the family of believers. Fear God, and respect the king" (1 Peter 2:17, NLT). The King at this point was Herod Agrippa—a man who accepted the praise of the people calling him a god, a man who harshly persecuted the early Church, a man who did great evil. *That* was the man Peter told the believers of his day to honor and respect.

The fact of the matter is this: God establishes every leader. But every leader established by God has the *choice* to submit to God's leadership and live and lead according to God's Kingdom. Sadly, many have failed. But this does not change our responsibility to come into alignment with our leaders. But it is also vitally important to understand that *alignment* is not always *agreement*. You can respect and submit to an authority figure without having to agree with everything they do and what they stand for. There are far too many people in our country that agree with this...until election year. I can't count how many times I've heard a new president called the "antichrist" by Christians that despise him. The utter lack of respect for authority, regardless of our agreement or disagreement with them, has become a deep issue that had begun to eat away at the witness of the Church. You can voice your disagreement. You can work to change the policies implemented by leaders. You can stand up for what is right in a workplace or school where it seems so much wrong is promoted. But everything you do must come from a place of honor and respect for the authorities God has placed in position.

When it comes to prayer, our effectiveness is also tied to our alignment. Don't get me wrong—God will always hear you and always has a willing disposition towards you. But you will limit yourself if you are not under proper alignment. Things like gossip, bitterness, offense, rebellion, and the like will push you further and further out of alignment. As a result, building the Kingdom becomes increasingly difficult with each step we take out of alignment. Think of a system of pipes. If you push a single pipe out of alignment, the result of the flow is affected. The more and more it comes out of alignment, the more and more the result is impacted. Do everything you can to understand God's plan for authority and then make sure you align yourself, or else you may find yourself at the end of your life wondering about what could have been!

Action Steps

1. This is a moment for serious, raw self-reflection. Take an objective look at your life and ask yourself how well you have honored and aligned under the authority God has placed in your life?

2. In my opinion, there is always room for improvement. We are always growing! So look at the examples where you missed the mark. Ask God to show you what you should have done to be in better alignment.

3. Repent from the errors, seek reconciliation with those you may have offense or bitterness with, and then work on steps to take to align your life with God's flow of authority better.

Week 5 - Day 6
Building the Kingdom
Healing

I think out of all of the gifts of the Spirit, the gift of healing is one of the most dramatic and impactful! To see a person with a cast, in pain, leave walking away from an encounter with Jesus without the cast or pain is nothing short of amazing. I have been incredibly blessed to be surrounded by men and women, mentors, and friends who have pursued this gift and have been used by God. I have seen several dramatic examples of the gift of healing in my ministry and the ministry of others:

I have seen a female youth student die on an operating table and come back to life. I have seen a woman in a wheelchair because of having MS for over 25 years stand up, get rid of her wheelchair, dance before the Lord in worship, and never return to the wheelchair. I have seen MRSA (a painful skin infection/disease) completely disappear from a young man's arm. I have seen multiple people healed of various kinds of cancer at varying stages. I have witnessed sore throats opened, chronic pain disappear, heart conditions healed, and torn ligaments mended. I have seen crushed, compressed, and slipped spinal disks and vertebrae realign and healed. Damaged cartilage, influenza, broken bones, chronic migraines, depression, eating disorders, sprains, hip issues, back issues, sickle cell anemia—all of it has bowed to the name of Jesus and His healing touch!

In every instance of legitimate healing I have seen, the person has been left knowing that God is real. While this is also true with many other gifts of the Spirit, it is all the more tangible with healing! There is no explanation for when a doctor who says your case is hopeless, and you will die, yet you receive healing and live a healthy life free of your ailment.

For some reason, though, so many people are skeptical of this gift! Many would even explain their lack of experience by saying that none of these gifts of the Spirit are available today—that somehow they were only meant for the Early Church. This is obviously nonsense.

When it comes to building the Kingdom "on Earth as it is in Heaven" (Matt. 6:10), healing is an essential element. First of all, to bring the realities of Heaven to Earth, we have to understand what those realities are. If sickness, pain, disease, and all of these other issues do not exist in Heaven, then we are mandated to make that a reality here as well. Secondly, we must understand that it is God's will to heal. Some people may want to disagree with me, but there is no way to pray with great faith without believing this!

Here are a few verses about God's heart to heal:

- *"Jesus called his twelve disciples to him and gave them authority to drive out impure spirits and to heal every disease and sickness" (Matt. 10:1).*

- *"When you enter a town and are welcomed, eat what is offered to you. Heal the sick who are there and tell them, 'The kingdom of God has come near to you'"* (Luke 10:8-9).
- *"...By his (Jesus') wounds we are healed..."* (Isaiah 53:5).
- *"...He sent them out to proclaim the kingdom of God and to heal the sick"* (Luke 9:2).

There are so many more verses that speak to God's heart to heal. We cannot allow our experiences of not seeing healing take place to determine our theology. A correct, contextual study of Scriptures will show that God's heart is always to heal!

The verse in Luke 9:2 (above) is especially telling. Not one Christian will disagree that God has commanded us to proclaim the Kingdom of God throughout the world. And yet, Jesus sent His followers to both proclaim the Kingdom of God and heal the sick. They go hand in hand. We cannot and must not separate them!

And the best part about this gift of the Spirit is that it is accessible to every single follower of Jesus! You can get up after reading this devotional, ask God to use you, go into the world, and see someone healed! It's not just possible or probably—it is most likely! Why? Because it is God's heart, His command, and He always backs up what He says!

Action Steps

1. Ask God to give you opportunities this week (even today) to pray for healing. Maybe He gives you a word of knowledge for an issue that He wants to heal. Maybe He paints a big proverbial bulls-eye on a person that is too obvious to miss! Be on the look-out. Be aware! If you need a faith booster, write down Scriptures dealing with God's heart to heal and read them over and over to strengthen your faith!

2. Be tactful! Introduce yourself, explain that you are a follower of Jesus and believe in healing, and ask if you can pray for them. If yes—go for it! If no—accept it and leave.

3. Pray with your eyes open to see what God may be doing. After praying, ask them to test what they could not do before (if possible).

Week 5 - Day 7
Building the Kingdom
Giving

*F*inances are typically one of the touchiest subjects when it comes to building the Kingdom of God. Why? Because we are possessive about our money. We work hard for our money. We live in a world that is controlled, dictated, and fueled by finances. Giving to one thing means taking it away from another. We exert control over our finances and refuse to give to anything that does not match our goals and values in life.

The Bible speaks a lot about the topic of finances. It teaches that the borrower is a slave to the lender (Proverbs 22:7), meaning that debt is bondage and is bad. The Bible tells us that the love of money is a root of all kinds of evil (1 Timothy 6:10). It instructs us in the principles of sowing and reaping. It teaches us that although we are no longer obligated under the Old Testament Law to give our tithe, we should willingly and cheerfully give it generously to God through our local church as a true act of worship. It also teaches us that the faithful giving of the followers of Jesus both provide for the Church as well as help advance and build God's Kingdom.

So why is this area so touchy? If the Bible is so clear on this matter, why do we struggle to give? Some people choose not to give, convincing themselves that there is a genuine reason to justify their decision. Others only give what they think they can spare (out of their excess). Others give sacrificially. Some people have been known to hold their giving hostage to get pastors to follow the giver's agenda for the church.

Why are there so many issues?

The answer is simple, yet profound: Our money represents our lives!

All of your time, energy, success, possessions, quality of life, career, priorities, achievements, etc. are touched by, if not downright dependent, upon the money you have and earn! For some, their bank account is, in a very real way, representative of their life's work. I'm not saying that your finances define you. Far from it! But how you spend your finances *does* reveal what is important to you in your life. And there is no way around this hard truth.

One of my favorite passages in the Bible about giving is found in Jesus' "Sermon on the Mount." During this teaching, Jesus says,

> *"'Do not store up for yourselves treasures on earth, where moths and vermin destroy, and where thieves break in and steal. But store up for yourselves treasures in heaven, where moths and vermin do not destroy, and where thieves do not break in and steal. For where your treasure is, there your heart will be also.'"[22]*

---

22 Matthew 6:19-21 (ESV)

This passage has single-handedly transformed our approach to giving as a family. According to Jesus, our treasures (which includes our finances, though not exclusively our finances) that we accumulate fall into one of two categories: temporal and eternal. Certain things that we choose to spend our finances on are temporary. There will come a day, either immediately, in the distant future, or somewhere in between when the temporary things we have invested in (our treasures) will fade away. They may even be temporary in the fact that they outlast our time on Earth, and we can no longer enjoy them once we die. The end result with temporary treasures is always the same: they are short-lived.

However, there are things we can invest our finances into that will have an eternal impact, leave a legacy, and store up rewards and treasures for us in Heaven. This happens when we decide to take our role as stewards of our finances and resources and begin to give towards building the Kingdom of God. Proving this point, Paul identifies one of the gifts of the Spirit as giving (Romans 12:6-8)!

If we could only understand that our giving is a spiritual act and not an obligatory act, there would be an incredible increase in the testimonies we see daily. If we could get to the place of understanding our giving as an act of deep, self-sacrificial worship instead of trying to justify why we don't give and why we aren't generous, we would see tremendous levels of freedom and breakthrough in our churches!

Don't settle for obligatory giving. Don't settle for trying to avoid the shame and guilt that our justifications for not giving bring. Don't settle for a life of complacency, especially in giving. And above all, don't settle with a lack of faith in God to provide! If giving is a spiritual gift that we can all function in, that would mean God has to provide income for you to give! Functioning properly in the gift of giving—with integrity and honor—will actually make you wealthy!

Lastly, consider the generosity of God. He has made Himself known to the world through generosity. He gave Himself to Mankind in various covenants. He has proven Himself faithful and long-suffering with every one of us. He sent His Son to live as one of us and to reveal the Father to us. And He gave His only Son to die a willing and sacrificial death for the sin of the world so that we could be brought back into right relationship with Him.

The Bible is pretty clear that God reveals Himself to the world through generosity—in love, forgiveness, finances, and relationship. If our goal is to imitate and follow Jesus, then we should offer our lives as living sacrifices (Romans 12:2)—even our finances—so that the world can know the incredible Father!

Action Steps

1. Sit down at some point this week and take a good hard look at every monthly budget/expense item you have—Put them into four categories: (1) Highly important (2) Important (3) Somewhat important (4) Not that important.

2. Once every expense is in its proper category, review them all. Seek God for how He wants you to steward your finances. You would be surprised what we find important and what we spend our money on that is not so important!

3. Ask God to speak to you about what you should be giving

to your local church, but also how to live a more generous lifestyle with those within your sphere of influence. It may be scary, but remember, God is faithful! Giving to our local churches and living a lifestyle of generosity is how we build the Kingdom of God through our finances!

RESOURCES

These resources are a great starting point for learning more about some of the individual topics talked about in this book

PRAYER & FASTING

Fasting	Jentezen Franklin
Fasting	Michael Dow
Intercessor	Rees Howells
Intercessory Prayer	Dutch Sheets
The Practice of the Presence of God	Brother Lawrence
The Lost Art of Intercession	James Goll

WALKING WITH GOD

Emotionally Healthy Spirituality	Peter Scazarro
Hosting the Presence	Bill Johnson
Static Jedi	Eric Samuel Timms

SPIRITUAL IDENTITY

141

TOOLS FOR DEVELOPING SPIRITUAL MATURITY

SABBATH

The Sabbath is not one day in your week that you do nothing. Sabbath is not merely rest from work/activity. Sabbath is a day-long rest from the rhythm of life to be able to enjoy God. God did not make the Sabbath for Himself, but for us—for our well-being! This day is sacred and should be protected. It should be intentionally planned out to a certain degree so that everything you do moves you towards the goal of resting and delighting in God.

Here are some ideas for how to rest on your Sabbath:
- Read
- Play with your kids
- Go out and enjoy time with your spouse
- Take a walk
- Read your Bible
- Listen to Music
- Don't answer your phone, text messages, etc

- Limit social media intake
- Leave work at the office
- Do the things that bring you joy

Sabbath is a day where you bring the rhythm of life to a halt so you can realign yourself with the rhythm of the Spirit. It is not legalistic in that you cannot do any activity, but what you do must allow you to delight in God, His creation, and life.

SPIRIT-LED BIBLE READING

A lot of people may tell you that you should have a Bible reading plan that helps you read through the entire Bible in 1 year. While this is not a bad idea, it can be ineffective when your approach is only to read the words of the Bible. Digging deeper wells does not depend on the number of words in the Bible that you read, but rather how we allow God to speak to us through those words!

There have been times when I have spent an entire month in the book of Colossians, while at other times, I have read through 1 & 2 Kings in a few weeks. Both were meaningful and impactful. The point is that you need to learn how to allow God to hear God's voice through scripture. Bible Reading is an experience, not homework!

There is a spiritual practice known in church history as *lectio divina* (divine reading). It is not a good practice for trying to interpret the Bible. It is useful, however, for allowing the Holy Spirit to speak to you through familiar texts. Here is a helpful process to start with:

1. Intentionally set aside some time in your day where you can focus and be undisturbed.

2. Ask the Holy Spirit which book of the Bible to start reading through.

3. Start reading. Be aware of the things that stick out to you— the words or statements that seem to jump off the page at you and grab your attention. Once that happens, finish the passage and then stop.

4. Spend some time thinking about what caught your attention. Allow the Holy Spirit to speak to you and guide you. Ask Him what it is that He is saying to you. Feel the emotions of the characters involved. Try to understand the situation. Try to understand the context of the text. This may require some further reading of the surrounding passages to really understand what is happening. Other times, you may be able to set certain things aside and ask your pastor later, who has studied more in-depth into the culture and history of the Bible. The text has one correct interpretation but can have multiple spiritual applications to your life.

5. Filter your thoughts and reasoning through the person of Jesus. He is perfect theology. The entire Bible points to Jesus, so it must be interpreted through who Jesus is. If your thoughts or reasoning does not match the nature of Jesus, then go back and re-think through the passage.

6. Once you feel like Holy Spirit has spoken to you, begin to thank God for His word. Affirm what He has spoken to you. Ask for His help and guidance. Don't be afraid to talk about your emotions—fear, joy, excitement, pain, offense, convictions, passions, etc. Prayer is communion with God.

7. Go over that message in your mind over and over again. Allow it to shape your thinking and to rid you of bad theology and lies about who you are. Allow God to speak life into you and change you.

8. Finally, think about how this message should affect your daily life and behavior. How will this help you move further in the areas you want to see growth? How will this change some of the ways you are living? How will this affect your decision-making? Then resolve yourself to live that way intentionally one day at a time until it becomes natural for you.

SILENCE & SOLITUDE

Silence and Solitude are so important in a world where we are over-stimulated and drowning in an endless ocean of information. With so many "voices" competing for your attention, it can become extremely challenging to be sensitive enough to hear the voice of God.

The goal of Silence and Solitude is to unclog your spiritual ears to be able to recognize the voice of God clearly and immediately. It is a short period of rest every day or multiple times a day that allows you to stop the constant flow of mental stimulation and allows your mind, body, soul, and spirit to adjust their frequency away from all the static and towards the Presence of God. This practice is a realignment of the gaze of your heart.

Here are some tips to help get you started:

- Don't start bigger than you can manage. Start with a set time frame that is realistic and manageable. Nothing will frustrate you more than trying to start at 30 minutes every day, but only being able to get 5 minutes because you have not identified the right daily rhythm.
- Pick the right time of day when you can be alone. It doesn't have to be a long time frame, but it should be undisturbed.
- Set your phone to "silent" so it does not become a distraction.
- Choose the right location! If your office or living room makes you want to work or clean or watch tv, then avoid those rooms. Find a space that allows you to focus. With time, you will get used to this level of focus and be able to handle different environments.

SOAKING

Soaking is somewhat similar to Silence & Solitude, but it has a different goal and method to it. We call it "soaking" because you are "soaking in His presence" like a sponge. When you engage in "soaking," you are placing yourself in an environment where you are aware of the Presence of God. Once you have become sensitive and aware to His Presence, you quiet yourself, remain still, and allow yourself to experience the peace, joy, and profound awareness of God with you at that moment. It is fully engaging in the moment.

In these moments, God may speak to you, give you visions, or bring you into an encounter with some facet of who He is as He reveals Himself to you in a deeper, more personal way.

Here are a few ways you can start this process today:

1. Dedicate 15 minutes in your schedule to be alone somewhere.

2. Turn off your phone and other devices you may have that can disturb you.

3. Put some soft worship music on.

4. Begin worshiping God, allowing praise and thanksgiving to flow from your heart.

5. Once you begin to sense His presence, continue to worship and praise Him.

6. When you feel like you are genuinely connecting to God and feel the weight of His presence, silence yourself and be still. Just set your heart and mind on Him. This moment is called "soaking" in His presence.

HABITUAL PRAYERS

This one may feel unspiritual, but is *far* from unspiritual! Habitual prayers are prayers that you pray throughout your day that are triggered by regular activity and habits. It is experiential prayer. We see this a lot in the profound movement of the Celtic Christianity of old.

Habitual prayers are prayers that you learn to pray at specific points in your day.

Example #1: When I wake up in the morning and step into the cool morning air, I pray something like this:

- *"God—thank you for the cool air that is filling my lungs and refreshing me. Just like the air, let your life fill my lungs and refresh my soul."*

Example #2: When I am getting dressed, I might pray:

- *"Father—as I am getting dressed, I want to thank you that you have clothed me in righteousness! I am not a sinner, saved by grace; I am the righteousness of God in Christ Jesus! Help me to see myself that way as I go about my day."*

You can pray habitual prayers during any regular activity. It is not an obligatory ritual, but a practice to help increase your awareness of the ever-present Holy Spirit in your midst. The more aware you are of Him throughout your day, the more spiritual growth you will experience. The trick of it is not to pray these prayers just to do them. You must intentionally focus on Him when you pray them.

SPIRITUAL RETREAT

Sometimes as believers, it is important to be alone with God for an extended time. The Bible tells us that Jesus would sometimes go up on a mountain by Himself to be with God for an extended time. We call this a spiritual retreat.

Spiritual retreats are a pre-planned break from your typical surroundings and business. It gets you alone with God for a pre-determined period to be able to pray, worship, study the Word, hear His voice, etc.

Here are some tips for planning a spiritual retreat:

- A spiritual retreat is not permission to ignore your responsibilities or the relationships in your life. If you are married, it is wise to agree together on the right season and time-frame.
- Find a secluded location: a hotel, cabin, campground, woods, a day-trip hike, spare room in a friend or family member's house, etc.
- Get anything pressing on your schedule done ahead of time so that you can truly disconnect and find peace and rest as you go on this retreat with God.
- Be open to the leading of the Holy Spirit. Leave your agenda behind. He has rarely revealed Himself to me in the way that I had intended and planned for Him to. He comes on retreats in the ways that we need Him to!

REST

Rest is not the absence of activity, but the presence of peace and calm *in the midst* of activity. Learning to live in a place of continual rest is difficult, especially in our culture today. Learning to rest allows you to respond according to how a mature follower of Jesus would to a situation, instead of quickly reacting emotionally to the situation.

To find, learn, and live in this place of rest, you can begin to practice multiple things:

- Maintain Sabbath as a non-negotiable priority
- Start your day with a brief time of silence and contemplation—asking God to help you be at peace and to have the mind of Christ.
- Intentionally schedule your day with short breaks in it to turn the gaze of your heart back to God.
- As you go throughout your day, be sensitive to the beauty of God's creation all around you. Open your spiritual eyes to see Him in His creation, His moving in the lives of others, and the ways that He is revealing His goodness.
- Intentionally schedule 1-2 day breaks in your work/activity calendar. Make sure these happen about every 3-4 months. During these days, try to do things that bring you peace and joy. These can be done with your family or without them. Scheduling these breaks in your schedule is not just practical, but spiritual as well!

BIBLE STUDY

Studying your Bible—not just reading it—is an essential part of your ability to dig deep wells in your life. The goal of studying your Bible is to understand what the biblical authors originally intended their writing to mean to their original audience—not what you think it means!

The Bible was written over several thousand years, to a world full of very different cultures, languages, and customs from what is normal to us in the 21st-century.

There are several tools you can use to help you study your Bible more effectively:

- Purchase a commentary: Commentaries are the thoughts, research, and interpretation of biblical passages from scholars who have done all of the "heavy lifting" for you. Not all commentators agree, but they will give you access to much more information than you currently have access to
- www.biblehub.com : This is an online bible study tool that gives you access to older commentaries, lexicons (a tool that shows you the original language of a text and interprets those languages into English), and multiple translations of the Bible. This tool takes time to master but is a great tool to use.
- Read a book or take a class about hermeneutics (the art and science of studying and interpreting scripture).
- You can purchase a teaching series on this subject from our "Renew Resources" page on our website: *www.renewmin.org*

HEARING GOD'S VOICE

There are special times when a person may hear the audible voice of God. However, it is also important to remember that God is not limited to our human languages. God's language takes on many different forms. He speaks in the tension and release of a beautiful piece of music. He speaks through the vibrant colors of the sunset. He speaks in the soft rustling of leaves in the trees. He also speaks through impressions, thoughts, images, the words of others, and dreams.

Here are some (not all) of God's ways that He speaks to us that you should start paying attention to:

1. Impressions
   - These are feelings, specific words, or images that God gives to you in a moment. They carry a deeper message and significance once you start asking Him for their meaning.

2. Thoughts
   - These are often random thoughts that pop into your head while you are praying/seeking Him. Not every random thought is from God. Many can simply be distractions. But many times, these thoughts can be from God about things He wants you to know, to do, to pray about, a direction He wants you to take, etc.

3. The Bible

- One of the easiest ways to hear from God is to open your Bible and start reading. Allow the message to penetrate your heart and speak to your life and situation. Read His promises and find comfort, peace, and joy. Find encouragement and strength from the apostles. God has given the Bible to us to reveal Himself to us. The whole Bible is one long narrative of God progressively revealing Himself to Mankind.

4. Other People

- Sometimes God places people in our lives so that He can speak through them to us. They may be aware that He is speaking through them, or they may not. They may be lovingly correcting, providing advice, encouraging, or prophesying into our lives. No matter how God does it, a mature follower of Jesus knows that it is wise to listen for the voice of God speaking through other believers.

5. Recurring Words/Pictures/Themes

- There are many times when the same word, picture, thought, or phrase will continually be in front of you. It keeps coming up on signs, in sermons, in conversations with friends, on commercials, etc. These may be God trying to grab your attention and have you pray about or act on something.

6. Dreams

- The Bible shows us that God speaks through our dreams. Dreams can be highly symbolic and very personal. Again, not every dream is from God, but the ones that are can be very significant for our lives. Symbolism in dreams are interpreted by either what they mean in the Bible, or what they represent to the dreamer. If you have a dream that you feel is from God, write it down as soon as possible in a journal with as much detail as you can remember. Pray about it over time, and ask God to reveal it to you. It may be about you, someone you know, or something about which God wants you to pray. Whatever it is, the purpose of your dreams may come to pass immediately, within a short time, or many years from now. Write it down so you can always go back to it and see God's faithfulness!

7. Seeing

- There are times when you might actually "see" things in life—on people, in a background, hear a sound, smell a particular fragrance. None of those things are there. Now, we are not talking about symptoms of mental illness or physical conditions. We are talking about legitimate spiritual communication from God. These are things that engage your sight but are not actually there. These things come with a "knowing"—an understanding as to what it means for you or for someone with whom you are interacting.

8. Creation

  • As we have already covered, God can speak to you through the beauty of His creation. The Bible states several times that the "heavens" (the sky, stars, etc.) declare God's praises. The Bible tells us that "all creation" testifies to the nature and goodness of God. Should it be any surprise that when you are out walking, on vacation, traveling, or going about your day that you happen to notice something about His creation that sticks out to you? Follow that thought and allow God to amaze you with how He speaks through your encounter with His creation!

FASTING

Fasting is denying your physical body sustenance to refocus your attention on God, connect with Him on a deeper level, and to accomplish a specific goal.

This list is not exhaustive, but some of the primary ones that we see in the Bible:

Types of Primary Fasts

1. "Day Fast"
  • Judges 20
  • Full Fast: No food or drink from sunrise to sunset.

2. "3 Day Fast"
   - Esther 4:16
   - Total Fast: No food or drink.

3. "21 Day Daniel Fast"
   - Daniel 10:2-3
   - Partial Fast: Only fruits, vegetables, and water.

4. "40 Day Fast"
   - Matthew 4
   - Liquid Fast: Only drink water.
   - This fast should be only done in consultation with a doctor as it can be dangerous if not done correctly.

For more details about the specifics of these and other types of fasts, refer to the "Resources" section provided in the back of this book.

ABOUT THE AUTHORS

 EJ and Darcie Martone are passionate about seeing people experience God through deep, intimate encounters in His presence, as well as through the demonstration of the power of the Spirit. Burdened by God with a desire to see lost spiritual orphans discover the loving embrace of their heavenly Father, EJ and Darcie, along with their six kids, have dedicated their lives to building the Kingdom of God here on Earth as it is in Heaven. They currently serve as pastors, writers, and communicators working to build the local church and to equip believers to live the life of the Kingdom.

ABOUT RENEW

RENEW

Renew Ministries is a ministry of EJ and Darcie Martone that seeks to be a catalyst for a deep spiritual renewal in a world that has fallen into the traps of apathy and dead religious activity. Renew works towards the advancement of the Kingdom of Heaven on Earth through equipping and training believers and leaders in the Church, both local and abroad. In an effort to supply this training, EJ and Darcie have also created Renew Resources, a collection of resources they have written or sponsored that will help any church and/or leader see the Kingdom advance in their church, community, and region.

For more information on Renew Ministries and to find Renew Resources, visit *www.renewmin.org*

MORE TITLES FROM EJ MARTONE

"Sons of Liberty"
Discovering Freedom Through the Father's Embrace

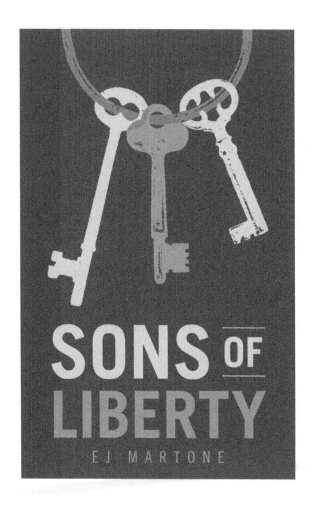

Made in the USA
Middletown, DE
04 January 2020